IF I WOULD HAVE DIED THAT DAY

JEFF BARDEL

Unless otherwise indicated, all Scripture quotations are from *The New King James Version.* Copyright © 1992 by Thomas Nelson, Inc. Used by permission. All rights reserved.

Scripture quotations marked ESV are from *The Holy Bible, English Standard Version.* Copyright © 2001 by Crossway Bibles, a publishing ministry of Good News Publishers. Used by permission. All rights reserved.

Scripture quotations marked KJV are from *The King James Version* of the Bible.

Scripture quotations marked NLT are from *The Holy Bible, New Living Translation.* Copyright © 2013 by Tyndale House Foundation. All rights reserved.

Scripture quotations marked TPT are from *The Passion Translation®.* Copyright © 2017, 2018 by Passion & Fire Ministries, Inc. Used by permission. All rights reserved. ThePassionTranslation.com

If I Would Have Died That Day
Copyright © 2020 by Jeff Bardel

Published in the United States of America

ISBN 13: 978-1-937250-61-4

1. Biography
2. Christian/Inspirational

TABLE OF CONTENTS

THE SOUND OF ONE HAND CLAPPING................... V

PREFACE... VII

1. SWIMMING POOLS AND GUARDIAN ANGELS.............. 1

2. A SUMMER JOB....................................... 5

3. THE DAY EVERYTHING CHANGED........................ 11

4. WORD STARTS TO SPREAD............................. 21

5. I REMEMBER MY EYES CLOSING........................ 29

6. DARK DAYS AHEAD................................... 35

7. PARKWAY DRIVES.................................... 41

   #TEACHABLEMOMENT—DO YOU LIKE WHAT YOU SEE?........... 43

8. A LIFE-CHANGING GAME OF PICK-UP BASKETBALL........ 47

9. A MISSIONARY FROM AFRICA.......................... 53

   #TEACHABLEMOMENT—GOD DIDN'T TAKE MY ARM.............. 56

10. MY NEW FRIEND, RICK.............................. 59

11. "WILL YOU SHARE YOUR TESTIMONY TONIGHT?"......... 63

12. "IF YOU WOULD HAVE DIED THAT DAY..."............. 69

   #TEACHABLEMOMENT—WAYS GOD SPEAKS..................... 74

#TEACHABLEMOMENT—How Can a Loving God Send People to Hell? . . 78

13. A New Love Interest 83

14. My Writing Career Begins 87

15. My Next Chapter 91

16. Sometimes Records Break 97
    #TEACHABLEMOMENT—When God "Speaks" 99
    #TEACHABLEMOMENT—Is Your Name in That Book? 101

17. Sometimes Records Break: The Sequel 109

18. My Challenge for You 117
    #TEACHABLEMOMENT—How Big Is Your "Want To" 118

The Sound of One Hand Clapping

👋 To my gorgeous wife, Kelli: thank you for all of your encouragement and patience while I locked myself away in the office at all times of the day or night to plug away at this book. You read and reread this more than anyone during the process. Your constant love, support, and belief in me is exactly what I needed to finish this project. I adore you, Dove!

👋 To my beautiful girls, Lily, Kenli & Tessa: thank you for giving me peace and quiet at least 50.1 percent of the time in our house while I typed away on my laptop. I love the role God allows me to play in your lives. I apologize for my frustrated days and pray my life reflects the pages of this book to you. I love you Lily Pad, Shae-Bone, and Bump!

👋 To my mom and stepdad, Phyllis & Robbie Clark: most of the pages in this book would have never happened if y'all hadn't been there with me in my darkest days. You cried with me, prayed with me, and loved me when I was my most unlovable. Thank you for everything! I love you, Gigi and Poppy!

👋 To my amazing sister, Christi Thompson: thank you for your research and editing help from start to finish. I've looked up to you my entire life, whether I've always admitted it or not. You've been a great example to follow (most of the time). I love you, Sissy!

👋 To the best grandparents I could have ever asked for, Erma & Grey Sewell: you were two of my favorite people on the planet and I miss you both every single day. I'd give anything for one more lunch together at Quincy's and for you both to read this book, but look forward to hugging you both on the streets of gold. I know they say there are no tears in Heaven, but I can't promise anything at that reunion. I love and miss you, Nini and Papa!

🖐 To my dad, Hank Bardel: I don't know if you ever believed me, but I never blamed my accident on you. You were just trying to help. I miss our rounds of golf together, and I'll see you on the other side. Love you, Pop!

🖐 To the many people who helped me the day of my accident: coworkers, EMTs, nurses, doctors, and the countless people who prayed for and encouraged me—everything you did mattered. I'm still here because of it. Thank you for doing your part!

🖐 To my many friends who read portions of this while I worked on it and gave me great feedback along the way, thank you from the bottom of my heart.

🖐 To my awesome Trailhead Church family: I appreciate all of your supportive words that I heard nearly every single Sunday while I worked on this project, even on those Sundays I didn't want to hear it. Thank you for the encouragement.

🖐 To my awesome graphic designer, JP Staggs: thank you for walking a rookie through this entire process and making it much easier than it actually is. (P.S. If you have any graphic design or book publishing needs, reach out to her at www.collipsis.com.) You're the best, Peege!

✝ To my Jesus: thank You for dying on the cross to save me from my sins. This is all for You!

Preface

It has long been a dream of mine to write a book. The first time I remember enjoying the gift of writing was when I was in the sixth grade. My teacher gave our class a homework assignment where we had to write a story. It could be about anything we wanted, but it had to be at least one page long.

When I got home from school, I plopped down at my desk and started writing. And I wrote...and wrote...and wrote. Before long I'd written four pages and the story had no ending in sight. It was about a family with 17 kids, and to this day, I still remember the names of three of them—Lele, Flefle, and Leleflefle. (And before you get all Judgey McJudgerson, I was a sixth grader, and my story was intended to be funny.)

The next day, our class broke up into groups of four, and we took turns reading our stories to each other. Then, we chose one of the four stories to be read to the entire class, and my story was chosen. I loved reading my story to my classmates. Hearing them laugh at a story I'd written made an impact on me. Writing became a part of who I was.

Fast forward a decade later when I started traveling and sharing my story, which you will read about in the coming pages. So many people approached me and told me I needed to write a book about my experience. In one respect, I loved the idea because maybe my story could encourage someone who was struggling. In another respect, it scared me because there were certain parts of my experience I didn't want to relive. They were too dark and painful.

In the last few years I developed a new motto that I live by. When I experience something negative, I don't ask, "God, why did this happen?" Instead, I ask, "God, how can You get glory from this?" So that's why I chose to write this, and I hope that's exactly what happens.

Now, there are a couple of things I want to tell you as you get ready to dive into the following pages. Over the years, my family and I were told many things that happened throughout the process of me losing my arm. From time to time, some of the information was slightly off or just completely wrong. As I wrote this book, if it wasn't something I personally remembered, my family and friends remembered, or it wasn't something I could find in a doctor's report or legal document, I didn't include it. I did this because I want this book to be as accurate as possible.

Also, as you read, occasionally you will see grayed out boxes with the hashtag #TeachableMoment at the top. There are moments throughout my story that lead to a teaching about a specific topic that I couldn't just gloss over. I decided to put them in gray boxes because they can be a bit of an interruption to the story. If you want to continue with the story, simply skip the gray box and keep reading. If you want to read them later, I've added each #TeachableMoment to the Table of Contents along with the specific title and page number for easy reference. If one of them really speaks to you, post your thoughts about it on social media with the hashtag #TeachableMoment and the title of the book. That way, together, we can reach more people.

So, here it is. My labor of love.

Enjoy,

Jeff Bardel

CHAPTER 1

Swimming Pools and Guardian Angels

When I was 18 years old, my life was forever altered by an experience I still remember in vivid detail. Certain smells, sounds, or even lighting can rip me from where I am and snatch me back in time — like Marty McFly in a Delorean — to the hot, dirty, glass factory where my life forever changed in a split second. I guess when you are not just in the fight of your life, but a fight *for* your life, it tends to remain fresh in your mind.

But, let's not get ahead of ourselves. Let's start at the beginning and work our way to the present.

I was born January 7, 1975, at 7:57 a.m. All of those 7s, however, didn't prove to be lucky as the doctors quickly discovered I had fluid in my lungs. I was only given a 50 percent chance at living. But I wasn't going to let any silly lung fluid keep me from gracing this earth with my presence. I survived that ordeal (obviously, as I'm not writing this from "the other side"), and the world rejoiced. Well, my family did.

The second, and more supernatural brush with death, happened when I was nine years old. My mom, 12-year-old sister, and myself were on a family vacation visiting some friends of ours in the great state of Louisiana. The friends we were visiting had two daughters who were eight and 11 at the time. Kids in that age range have an amazing knack for breaking things when cooped up in a house long enough, so after a few days we were escorted to the local public swimming pool where something immediately caught my eye. And no, it wasn't a girl. I was still trying to decide if they all had "cooties" or not. At that age, I figured at least 56 percent must have them, so I couldn't risk it. Anyway, what caught my eye was the high-dive.

To a nine year old, a high-dive looks *really* high, but I was always a bit of a daredevil. If you don't believe me, one of my dad's favorite stories he always told of me as a youngster was the time he had to get his ladder to retrieve my bike from a low-hanging tree limb after an unsuccessful Evel Knievel impersonation.

That day at the pool after I took my shirt off and flexed my nine-year-old guns for the 44 percent of cootie-less girls at the pool, I sprinted toward the high-dive. I didn't care that the lifeguard blew his whistle at me. Actually, I did, so I showed off my speed-walking skills until I reached the base of the behemoth.

As I ascended the ladder, I used a little-known, seldom-used form of ladder climbing. I would grab one rung with both hands and pull up one foot at a time until they were on the same rung. Once both feet were secure, I would let go *with both hands* and reach for the next rung. (That step is why this form of ladder climbing is seldom used.) I utilized this technique until I reached the top of the ladder, where I would impress all onlookers (okay, basically just the lifeguard) with a multitude of dives (okay, basically I just jumped off and flailed one arm while I squeezed my nose shut with the other but it looked good).

I spent the remainder of our time at the pool that day climbing the ladder, flying through the air, splashing into the water, swimming to the side of the pool, and then speed walking back to the ladder. That's a pretty great day for a nine year old!

As the sun started to set in the west and the sky turned a brilliant orange, I was rushing to get in as many jumps as possible. I don't know about you, but when I go swimming, I have a tendency to get wet. Wet hands mixed with a nine year old trying to hurry up a ladder using an ill-advised climbing technique typically leads to an accident. And it nearly did.

On my final ascent of the day, I reached with both hands for the top rung of the ladder. When I did, my hands slipped and I started to fall toward the concrete 20 feet below. My feet were still on the rung, but my back was nearly parallel to the ground — Keanu Reeves' *Matrix* style — when it happened.

The only way I can explain it is that "something" caught me and pushed me back up. The next thing I knew, my hands were wrapped around the top rung, my entire body was shaking, and my mind was racing. My first thought: *Man, I've got some strong toes!* My second thought: *Don't tell Mom because I might get in trouble.*

After jumping off the high dive that final time, I swam over to the edge of the pool, climbed out, wrapped myself in a towel, and sat with our parents until it was time to go. I knew something had happened. I couldn't explain it. I was still shaken from what I'd experienced and confused as to what stopped my fall.

Nearly 10 years passed before I told my mom that story. And no, I didn't get into trouble. But when I get to Heaven, I can't wait to give the biggest high-five Heaven has ever seen to my guardian angel for showing up that day at the pool, and apologize for keeping him so busy my entire life.

CHAPTER 2

A SUMMER JOB

In July 1993, I had recently graduated high school. Some people graduate *magna cum laude*. Others graduate *summa cum laude*. I, however, graduated *thank you, laude*. I was a good student, but got bored easily. I spent many days in English class trying to write with my left hand, something that would come in handy later that year.

During the summer between my high school graduation and my first year of college, I was working two jobs. How else was I supposed to afford gas for my sweet ride? She was a maroon 1988 Pontiac Grand Prix LE. I wasn't sure what the "LE" stood for, so I always told everyone it meant "Limited Edition." One of the perks that set my beautiful car apart from the others was the door handle. Mine didn't sit below the window like everyone else's did. Mine sat next to the window, perpendicular to the ground. That was some fine American craftsmanship right there!

When you grow up in a small town with nothing to do, you spend a lot of time cruising. If you're unfamiliar with the term, it basically means driving up and down the same road over and over again, windows down, music blaring, and waving at all of the other cars doing the exact same thing. In my town, everyone cruised Main Street. On one end you turned around at a gas station and on the other, the Harris Teeter grocery store. And when you got bored, you sat in the Burger King parking lot until the cops came by and told you to move it along. We would do this for hours. Ah, the joys of small-town living!

When you cruised that much, it burned a lot of gas, thus my need for two jobs (not to mention my upcoming freshman year of college). One of the jobs, which I had been working for more than two years, was at Taco Bell. I was the annoying guy at the drive-thru window barking over the speaker, "Welcome to the Border, can I take your order?"

Although I'd been working there for quite some time, the pay wasn't very good...even with a 10-cent raise after working there for only six months. So when my dad told me the glass factory he worked at was looking to hire some help for the summer, I asked him how much they were paying. When his answer was nearly double what I was currently making, my response was, "When do I start?"

When I showed up for my first day at the glass plant, I soon realized seven other sons had taken their parent's offers to work the rest of their summer at the factory. Little did we know the kind of back-breaking labor we had gotten ourselves into.

Our first day on the job, after a short orientation, we found ourselves in the "hot end" of the plant. They called it the hot end because it was hot (creative, huh?). And when I say hot, I mean hot! Like *really* hot. Like hotter-than-the-hinges-of-the-gates-of-Hell hot. We weren't allowed to wear any kind of metal jewelry because it would heat up to the point it would actually burn our skin.

The hot end held all of the furnaces used in the glass-making process. I'm nowhere near a glass-making expert, but from what I understood the newly-made glass was run through a furnace, and if there were any imperfections in the glass, it would shatter and fall to the floor.

Well, someone had to clean it up.

Why not the eight soon-to-be college students? So on day one, we found ourselves at the edge of the 2850-degree furnace on our knees with 10-foot rakes raking out all of the broken glass. Once it was clear of the furnace, we dropped our rakes, picked up shovels, and loaded the debris into bins for recycling. At this point, I was thinking *Making tacos and burritos at Taco Bell is so much easier than this.*

By the end of my first day I was wondering what the heck I'd gotten myself into. But quitting wasn't even an inkling of an option. My dad told me in no uncertain terms after I'd been hired, "It took me 23 years to earn a good reputation out here. Don't ruin it in one summer."

"Yes sir."

Days two through eight were just as grueling as day one. It compared to being stuck in the movie *Groundhog Day* on the hardest-working day of your life. Early arrival to the factory, back-breaking work, lunch break, more back-breaking work, and then quittin' time. By the time I got home, I had enough energy to shower, eat, and fall asleep on the couch.

I was so excited when the weekend arrived because I'd have a couple of days to recuperate and hang out with my buddies between my shifts at Taco Bell before I was back at it early Monday morning. But that was before I was asked if I wanted to work any overtime on the weekend. My first thought was *You've got to be kidding me. I can barely walk now as it is.*

They followed their question with an explanation of overtime pay. Then my first thought was *What time do I need to be here Saturday?* My second was *I need to find someone to cover my shift at Taco Bell.*

After finding someone to work my Saturday shift, I put in eight hours at the glass plant and all eight of us took Sunday off because at that point we looked, smelled, and walked like the zombies on *The Walking Dead*—not to mention I had to sling some tacos on Sunday.

The following Monday and Tuesday were more of the same from the week before. I had gotten very used to staring into a blazing-hot furnace with a rake in my hand. So when we showed up to the job on day nine, I was pleasantly surprised when they told us we'd be working in a different area of the plant.

We left the hot end and made our way to an area of the factory called the silos. This was where the entire glass-making process started. And although it was much cooler, it was quite possibly the dirtiest area of the plant (and maybe planet) I'd ever seen.

Everywhere you looked there was an off-white powder that coated everything. And when I say everything, I mean *everything*. It was everywhere. On the walls. On the ceiling. On the floor. On the machinery. On the stairs descending into the bottom of the silos. The black door leading out to the train shed was discolored to the point it looked like the hull of a shipwrecked barge that had capsized and been at the bottom of the ocean for years. To reiterate, the powder was *everywhere*!

Well, someone had to clean it up.

And that's exactly what we were told we'd have to do. Thankfully, we didn't have to clean it off of every surface because that would've been like someone taking us to the beach and saying, "You see all of this sand? Yeah, I'm going to need you to clean that up."

Our task was to clean it off the floor, especially the areas where the other employees walked. Over the years of people continually walking on the powder, it had packed down and actually caked together. There were places where it was inches thick on the floor.

We were handed shovels and told to bust the caked-up powder into chunks, load it into wheelbarrows, and cart the debris from our job site to a machine called a screw auger nearly 50 yards away. When we arrived at the machine, we pushed the wheelbarrow up a ramp in order to dump the contents into the auger's hopper.

For those of you who don't know what a screw auger is, it's basically a giant screw inside of a tube with a funnel, known as a hopper, that sits on top of it. You dump whatever material you're cleaning or moving into the hopper. As the debris funnels into the tube, it gets caught in the threads of the giant rotating screw. As the screw turns, the debris gets forced up the tube and out of the distribution chute on the opposite end.

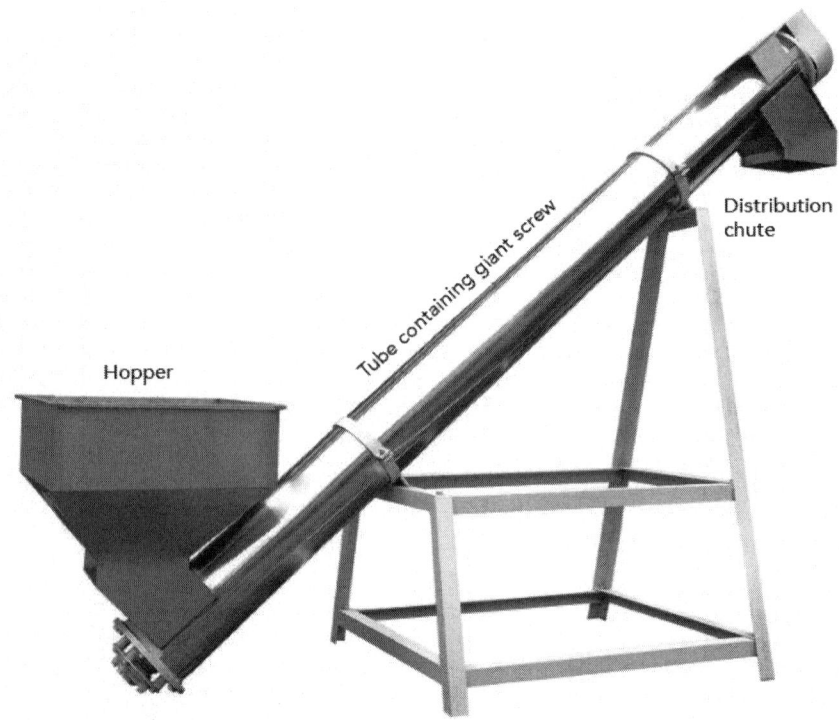

Diagram of a screw auger

The screw auger we worked with that day

With shovels and brooms in hand, we got to work. You have to remember this was the middle of July in North Carolina. The temperature outside was near or over 100 degrees, and we were required to wear jeans, steel-toed boots, and respirator masks to prevent us from inhaling too much of the powder. In a matter of no time, we were all covered in sweat. And when you're stirring up an off-white powder when you're covered in sweat, it didn't take long before the eight of us looked like ghosts haunting the bottom of the silos.

Any time the full-time employees saw our crew walking through the factory, we were laughed at more often than not. The veterans really enjoyed laughing at us rookies. But we never heard laughter from them quite like we did the day we walked into the lunch room after spending the morning working in the silos. I guess we looked more like Casper the Friendly Ghost.

After lunch, we went back to the job site and finished out our shift. I hadn't yet decided which was worse—the heat of the hot end or the dirtiness of the silos. I didn't know which job site we'd be working the next day, and I didn't really have a preference. I also didn't know how my life was about to drastically change.

CHAPTER 3

THE DAY EVERYTHING CHANGED

When I woke up the morning of July 22, 1993, I *really* didn't feel like going to work. I'd worked nine consecutive days, sometimes both jobs on the same day. My throat was sore, and my college orientation at Appalachian State University was only four days away. I didn't want to be sick when I went for my visit, so I was very close to calling out that day.

But my dad's warning still echoed in the back of my mind, "It took me 23 years to earn a good reputation out here. Don't ruin it in one summer." So I crawled out of bed and trudged into work.

I still remember what I wore that day. Actually, nearly everything about July 22, 1993, is still etched in my mind in vivid detail. For that shift I was wearing a pair of ratty blue jeans with my black steel-toed boots, a black Los Angeles Raiders hat with silver lettering, and a white Scotland High School baseball T-shirt with blue lettering that had a hole toward the collar (before you get all judgy, I wasn't walking the red carpet...I was cleaning a nasty factory). I played baseball while in high school and always wore the number 4, and that day I had on my gold rope necklace with a #4 pendant hanging from it.

When I showed up to work on day 10, we were back at the silos cleaning the caked-up powder off the floor. There were four different tasks we could be assigned to do. One was having a shovel in our hands busting up the debris on the floor and loading it into a wheelbarrow. Two was running the wheelbarrow back and forth from the job site to the screw auger. Three was standing at the base of the auger making sure all of the debris went down into the machine properly. Or four was waiting at the opposite end of the auger by the distribution chute. The powder that fell out of the chute went into a dumpster, so we had to take a shovel or rake to push the debris to the back of the dumpster so it didn't pile up under the chute.

From the moment we started working, I either had a shovel in hand busting up the debris and loading it into a wheelbarrow or I'd been running the wheelbarrow back and forth to the auger. One of my coworkers (and I use the term "coworker" *very* lightly), must not have gotten a motivational speech from his dad about his reputation because his work ethic was far from ethical.

Each day we'd shown up for work, our supervisor would explain our job to us for that shift, and we typically wouldn't see him again until we showed up for work the following morning. My coworker figured this out quickly and spent the majority of his time "supervising," which basically meant he watched us work whenever he wasn't napping.

So on our second day in the silos, when the supervisor left, this guy grabbed a chair, leaned it up against the wall, and attempted to take a nap. The rest of us were unusually loud for the first part of that shift for that very reason. But eventually we settled into our groove and forgot all about him.

Before long it was time for our lunch break and our "supervisor" was sound asleep. When you're wearing yourself out doing back-breaking work while this guy is sleeping (but still making the same amount of money as you), it kind of gets on your nerves. This feeling was shared by the rest of our crew, and some of them formed a plan.

His chair was leaned up against the wall with the two front legs off the ground. His feet—and more importantly, his boots—were dangling near the front legs of the chair, so two of my coworkers untied his boots, wrapped his laces around the legs of the chair, and tied his boots again. To be more accurate, they double-knotted his laces...snugly.

Once they were finished, we all went to the door. One guy yelled his name to let him know we were leaving for lunch, and we waited and watched. He pushed the chair away from the wall, stood up, and when he went to take a step he face-planted on the floor of the silos. The seven of us erupted in laughter and left for lunch while Sleepy Smurf figured out how to free himself from his entrapment.

The rest of us were already sitting down eating before he finally walked in the lunchroom. We all started laughing again, because what was the guy going to do, tell on us?

"I was taking a nap on the job when the guys who were actually working tied my boot strings around the chair I was asleep in, causing me to fall when I stood up to go to lunch. They should be disciplined!"

There are a couple of other things I remember about lunch that day: I ate fried chicken and definitely no vegetables. My guess is that I ate some version of potato (either mashed or fried) and/or some corn. Nothing green for sure unless it was candy. I also remember my dad ate with me. He didn't eat with me every day, but he did that day. He commented about my holey shirt, noticing my #4 pendant sat perfectly framed by the hole in my tee. Little did we know that when we said goodbye after lunch, the next time we saw each other would be under *very* different circumstances.

After returning to the job site, all eight of us got to work. Apparently, our "supervisor" learned his lesson because he picked up a shovel as well.

All of us switched from the jobs we'd been doing previously. I now found myself standing at the base of the screw auger. As a reminder, my job responsibility now was to make sure the debris went into the machine properly instead of clogging up in the hopper. The interesting thing is we weren't told what to do if the machine did get clogged up.

Another *very* important detail that was left out was the fact that all—yes, A-L-L, all—of the safety equipment had been removed from the machine. There were supposed to be emergency stop cables that ran the length of the machine. These were in place so that if anything went wrong, one quick pull of the cable and the auger would turn off immediately. Apparently, when the factory bought the auger from a nearby farm, the cables didn't make the trip.

There was also supposed to be a grating that covered the opening of the hopper to prevent any body parts or clothing from getting caught in the threads of the auger. It had been removed—whether by the farm or factory is still unclear—to make the process faster, because with the grating in place, the debris had to be broken into much smaller pieces.

I was waiting at the auger for the first load to be delivered, when I saw the tall, lanky frame of one of my coworkers pushing the wheelbarrow in my direction. His name was Preston Rainer and he was more of a friend than a coworker. We'd played baseball together since we were old enough to wear baseball gloves. "Pres" *really* liked me because he hit only one home run in his entire baseball career, and yours truly was the pitcher who served up the gopher ball.

And he *loved* to bring up that story, like it was the longest four-bagger ever hit in the history of the game. But, in all actuality, the ball literally bounced off the top of the fence in left field. A decent outfielder could have caught it (and our left fielder was *far* from decent...not that I'm bitter or anything), but nevertheless, it was a home run and he *never* let me live it down.

Anyway, Pres maneuvered the wheelbarrow up the ramp and dumped its contents into the hopper perched on top of the auger. He quickly wheeled around and returned to the job site. When I looked inside the hopper, most of the debris had funneled into the shaft and was working its way toward the dumpster.

There was, however, one larger piece of debris that was bigger than the rest. I could tell the auger was still turning beneath the clod of caked-up powder, but it was too large to fall into the shaft of the machine.

Again, we weren't told what to do if the debris backed up. We were just told to make sure it went down okay. I looked around for a shovel or rake I could use to force the piece further into the auger, but there weren't any at my job site. Knowing that my job was to ensure everything went into the auger properly, I decided to grab the large piece of debris by hand, break it on the floor, and put the smaller pieces back into the hopper. (Even as I'm writing this book at my kitchen table, I just heard some of you gasp.)

We were required to wear gauntlet gloves for safety reasons (oh, the irony), which were like regular gloves but they flared out at the wrist. When I grabbed the large piece of debris, something grabbed me. I felt a tug and immediately jerked back as hard as I could. My left arm came out fine. My right arm didn't.

The thread of the auger barely caught the corner of the glove on my right hand and cinched it tight around my wrist. I yanked frantically to try to free my hand but to no avail.

The remnants of my glove still caught
in the threads of the auger

The auger was rotating down and away from me, so my arm got pulled into the machine and slowly wrapped around the large metal screw inside the shaft. I remember the excruciating pain as my wrist dislocated, followed by the sheer agony of hearing and feeling my forearm snap.

I started screaming louder than I'd ever screamed before and for multiple reasons. First, the pain was absolutely unbearable as my arm continued to be fed to the machine. Second, I wanted someone to turn the machine off because I had been lifted from the ground and was being pulled into the hopper.

I had to scream at the top of my lungs because our job site was terribly loud. A large industrial conveyor belt dissected the basement of the silos and rumbled like thunder off the walls. You couldn't hear the person talking next to you unless they put their mouth next to your ear.

Another coworker by the name of Jonathan Hester was within earshot of me. He heard my screams and when he turned around, the upper portion of my body had disappeared into the hopper. With my left arm I was hanging on for dear life, trying to slow my descent as the unrelenting pull on my right arm kept inching me deeper into the auger's teeth. By the time Jonathan turned the machine off, both of my shoulders were dislocated—my right from the pull of the auger, my left from hanging on to the outside of the machine—and my neck was wrenched at an extremely awkward angle from the way my head turned as I was pulled into the funnel.

My left hand had a death grip on the rim of the hopper, so I pulled myself free from the machine's clutches as best I could with a dislocated shoulder. When my feet hit the ground, I pointed to where my right arm should have been. It was gone just above my elbow. I saw things you'd never want to see while watching a movie, much less experience in real life.

Jonathan stared at me for a few seconds before yelling, "Follow me!" He then turned and ran away. I was thinking *Dude, where are you going? I've got one arm here!* I didn't know where he was headed but I knew I didn't want to be by myself, so I took off after him. Without saying anything, we both knew that if I stayed there, I probably wouldn't survive.

In sheer terror and desperation, I sprinted through the basement of the silos, leaving a trail of blood along the floor and wall with each stride. As I ran I remembered an office about half of a football field away. I knew that if I could make it there, someone would be able to help me or at least I could get to a phone to call 911.

I reached a flight of stairs and took them two at a time, right on the heels of Jonathan who was going to the office as well. At the top of the stairs was a discolored metal door that my friend shoved open as I darted through. Another 10 yards and I found myself staring through the window into the silo operator's office.

I'll be honest, I had never had my arm ripped off by a machine before. I'd never even read a book on what to do if your arm got ripped off by a machine (after reading this, you won't be able to say the same), so I *really* didn't know what to do. I was obviously in a state of shock, so when I arrived at the office, I just stood in front of the window with a blank stare on my face. I didn't knock on the window. I didn't open the door and ask for a Band-Aid. I just stood there staring.

Three guys were in the office, and thankfully they saw me. Two of the guys said they couldn't go to me because they couldn't handle the sight of blood. So one called for help while a man named Joe Dew rushed out to help. As soon as he reached me, training from one of his former jobs as a bouncer kicked in. He put one hand on my chest and the other on my back and forced me to the ground. That might seem unnecessary, but he later told me, "I was scared that if I didn't get you on the ground you would run off because you were in total shock."

Once I was secured on the floor, Joe yelled at his coworkers who were still in the office to get paper towels to help him slow my blood loss. Apparently the guy in the office was in just as much shock as I was because he pulled a single paper towel from a roll on the wall, reached his hand out the door, and handed it to Joe.

Within seconds, the paper towel was completely soaked through, so he yelled that he needed more. Again, a single paper towel was handed through the door. He screamed, "GIVE ME THE WHOLE ROLL!" (Well, that's the edited version of what he said, anyway.) His coworker proceeded to rip the entire roll—dispenser and all—off the wall and shoved it to him from behind a barely-opened office door.

Joe proceeded to wrap the end of what was left of my arm in paper towels until more help arrived. He told me I kept repeating, "I'm going to die!" He tried to console me saying, "No you're not," but on the inside was saying *Please God don't let me be lying to him*. (There will be much more about Joe later in the book.)

One of the next people who reached me was actually the last baseball coach I ever had. His name was Don Dean and he played a key role in saving my life that day. He was over in the main part of the plant when he received a page telling him to get to the silos. As he was leaving his office, a maintenance man was driving by in a cart. He asked for a ride and hopped in as they rushed to where I was. Upon arrival, he saw me lying on the floor and prayed, "Lord, You've got to help us."

Don immediately knelt down beside me and placed his left knee firmly up against the right side of my face. It might sound like an awkward position, but he was very strategic in doing so. Because of the proximity of his knee to my right cheek, I couldn't turn my head to the right even if I wanted to (which I didn't).

I found out later he did that for two reasons. One, he knew I'd already seen enough. Not to sound overly graphic, but once you've seen your own jagged bone and torn flesh where your arm used to be, you've seen enough. Two, he didn't want me to see what he was about to do. He reached under my right armpit and squeezed absolutely as tight as he could, something he learned from his service in the United States Navy. He was attempting to slow my blood loss by acting as a human tourniquet, and at the rate my body was gushing it out, every last drop was critical. Remember, I had just finished a 50-yard sprint that would have made Usain Bolt jealous, so my heart was pumping it out much faster than normal. Honestly, I was in so much pain I don't even remember feeling Don's death grip under my dislocated shoulder.

By now, word was spreading throughout the plant about my accident and anyone with the ability to help was racing to the silos as quickly as possible. My dad was one of those people. He was in a meeting in the front office when someone ran in and reported that one of the college students had been hurt in the silos. He didn't wait to hear, "Meeting adjourned." He was on his feet and in a full sprint while those words still echoed off the conference room walls.

He slammed through a set of double doors facing the road that led to the silos, and as he did, he prayed a quick prayer and received an even quicker response.

"Please, God, don't let it be Jeff," was the cry of a desperate father hurrying to the site of an unknown accident to an unknown victim.

The soft words he heard in return froze him in his tracks, "Who do you want it to be then?"

He knew then he was rushing to the scene of his only son's accident.

Another gentleman in the same meeting with my dad was Cold End Supervisor Judson Smith. At the time, he was also an emergency medical technician for the local rescue squad. When he heard of an amputated arm in the silos, he grabbed his rescue radio, which he always carried on his hip, and radioed emergency medical services to have an ambulance dispatched. He knew every minute was absolutely critical, especially during the "golden hour," which is the first 60 minutes after a severe injury. By using his radio instead of calling 911, he saved a few precious minutes.

And he saved more than minutes that day.

My dad and Judson sprinted the distance of a football field from the front office to the silos, Judson trailing my father by about 20 yards. When they arrived at the silos, they both ran within 10 feet of the auger, unaware the remnants of my right arm were inside. I couldn't see either of them yet because I still had a knee plastered to my right cheek, but as they entered the silos, they heard someone yell from behind them, "We have to open this auger up and get his arm out!"

I was staring up at the ceiling when my dad's face appeared over the shoulder of my baseball coach, who was kneeling by my head talking to me in an effort to keep me conscious. My dad screamed an obscenity before hurling a Randy Johnson-like fastball with his work pager into the opposite wall of the silo, shattering the pager into more pieces than my shattered arm.

When our eyes made contact, we each saw fear like we'd never seen before. I watched as my dad stood motionless before walking away from me for a few seconds.

Judson raced up on the scene and was forced into a decision immediately—a decision that could forever change my life. He had to decide whether or not to apply an actual tourniquet to my mangled arm. That might seem like an easy, no-brainer decision, but Judson knew the long-term implications. If he applied a tourniquet, there would be zero hope of reattaching my arm because of the damage my capillaries and tissues would undergo. He didn't know the condition of my arm that was still twisted inside the threads of the auger. But the massive puddle of blood next to my right side forced his hand.

I watched as he started taking his belt off. I was thinking *Hang on, it's not that kind of party!*

He wrapped his belt near the shoulder above my mauled arm and cinched it as tight as he possibly could. I was already in extreme pain, but I do remember feeling the tourniquet. The pressure. The squeezing. The discomfort.

Once the tourniquet was in place, Judson grabbed his rescue radio again, squeezed the call button, and said, "Get me a bird in the air." A Life Flight helicopter was en route shortly thereafter to the hospital where I'd soon be transported via ambulance.

After Judson was in position, Don relinquished his title of human tourniquet and resumed a title he'd held for a long time: Hank Bardel's friend. He raced to my dad's side and said, "Hank, get down on the floor and talk to him. Jeff needs you, buddy. Keep him conscious."

After gaining his composure to the best of his ability, my dad hustled over, knelt down by my left shoulder, reached for my hand, and said these words, "Let's pray." Lying on the dirty floor staring up at my dad, we said The Lord's Prayer together. At this point my fingers were dug deep into my dad's forearm, because when he reached for my hand, I also reached for his and we both overshot our intended goal. There were five distinct bruises on his left forearm that lasted well into my hospital stay.

Judson began to gather as much information as possible — allergies, any current medications I was taking, blood pressure — before the EMTs arrived to save any time he could.

At 1:49 p.m., an ambulance's reverse warning echoed throughout the train shed attached to the silo as it backed up to my prone body. EMTs checked my vitals, started an IV, loaded me onto a gurney, and slid me into the back of the ambulance.

My dad was bound and determined to ride in the back of the ambulance with me, but Judson, who knew of my dad's cardiac issues, said we wouldn't move until he got off. When my father pressed, Judson said, "Hank, I know about your heart problems. We can't have you in the back with us in case you have a heart attack." My dad reluctantly climbed out of the ambulance and we sped off for the five-mile drive to Scotland Memorial Hospital.

CHAPTER 4

Word Starts to Spread

If you're from a small town, you know how quickly news spreads, especially bad news. A high school friend of mine referenced my accident as the JFK of the class of 1993, because everybody remembers where they were when they first heard the news. Within a few hours, the news of my accident had spread all the way across the country to a friend who was playing in a golf tournament in California at the time, and, remember, this was before the days of cell phones and social media.

My mom and stepdad, Phyllis and Robbie Clark, were at home. Most of their furniture was either on the front porch or in the front yard. No, we weren't *that* kind of home. They were having new carpet installed throughout the house, so everything was outside.

The phone rang and my mom answered. She heard my dad's voice on the other end of the line. His first words were, "Phyllis, is somebody there with you?" When she answered yes, he said, "You need to sit down." She sat down and he told her I'd been in an accident. She was in shock.

"Jeff's arm has been severed," she heard.

"What do you mean his arm has been severed?"

"His arm is gone."

"What do you mean his arm is gone?"

The man installing carpet in my parent's house could only hear my mom's side of the conversation, but later told his boss that he had to walk outside because he was scared he was going to get sick all over the freshly-installed carpet.

After my mom hung up the phone, she immediately called a fellow church member to start a prayer chain. She didn't know what my exact condition was or whether my arm could be reattached, but she did know I needed all the prayers I could get.

A few minutes later, my mom and stepdad were speeding down the road to get to me. They were confused and still in shock, so they drove to the glass factory, not knowing I had already been whisked away in an ambulance. When they reached the gate to the plant, they were informed by the security guard that I was no longer there, so off they sped to the local hospital.

Upon arrival, they immediately were taken back to me in the emergency room. Although I was freezing from the loss of blood and in excruciating pain, I felt comforted knowing my mom was in the room.

While I was on the table writhing in pain waiting for the helicopter to arrive, my mom told me my grandparents were in the waiting room and wanted to see me. I was very close to my Nini and Papa. On a few occasions as a kid, I'd go over to their house to spend the night and end up spending a whole week. And everyone knew my Papa and I had a special relationship. Growing up, I was often referred to as his shadow, because wherever he was, I was typically right behind or beside him. My seat at church or at a restaurant was always next to him. This is the man who not only never missed one of my baseball games, but he never missed a practice.

So, when I was told they wanted to see me, the only thought that went through my head was *I can't let them worry about me*. When my grandparents walked into the room, Papa came over and grabbed my left foot. I looked at him, smiled, and said, "Don't worry, Papa, I'll be out there swinging a bat again in no time." He never said a word (very typical of my Papa). He just smiled at me, squeezed my foot, and turned to walk out of the room with Nini close behind.

Because of all the commotion going on in my room with nurses scurrying around and my parents standing close by, I couldn't actually see if my grandparents were out of the room yet. I remember asking a few times to anyone who would listen, "Are they gone? Are they gone? Are they gone?"

Once I was assured they could no longer see or hear me, my writhing and moaning commenced.

When the helicopter arrived, I was loaded onto a gurney and wheeled out to my flying chariot, my parents walking right next to me. It was at that moment I realized I was being taken to Duke University Medical Center.

For those of you who don't already know, I'm a huge North Carolina Tar Heel fan, so the absolute last place on earth I ever want to be taken is Duke University! I mean, they already root for the devil. I don't care if it's a blue devil, green devil, red devil, or yellow devil. A devil's a devil! But, I figured if they could reattach my arm, I'd at least say, "Thank you." I still wouldn't pull for their basketball team, but I'd be appreciative.

I do remember making one request before I was loaded onto the helicopter. The medicine they were giving me for the pain made my nose itch constantly. I only had one arm, and it was covered in IV and oxygen tubing, so I didn't have the ability to scratch my own nose. Because of the fear and agony I was in, I kept hyperventilating as well, so my nose and mouth were covered by an oxygen mask.

Before the mask was put into place, however, I asked the emergency room nurse to tell whoever was going to be on the helicopter with me to scratch my nose. I was already in terrible pain, so there was no sense in having an itchy face, too. The message either wasn't delivered or wasn't heeded because for the duration of the flight, my nose was scratched three times tops.

The worst part was the fact that I couldn't even ask the Life Flight nurse to scratch my nose because of the mask covering the bottom half of my face. Even if I screamed from under the mask, the chopping of the helicopter blades would drown out my cries. I figured the only way to free myself from the oxygen mask to ask for assistance was to violently shake my head back and forth. My plan worked, but the nurse thought I was panicking, not trying to ask for a little scratch of my snout, so when she saw the mask out of place, she quickly grabbed it, put it back in position, and told me to calm down and take deep breaths.

Are you kidding me? Will you please, for the love of God, just scratch my freaking nose!?!?

The flight took a total of one hour and 35 minutes, 25 minutes shorter than a car ride. It actually took 35 minutes longer than expected because the pilot had to avoid two thunderstorms. The way my day was going, I'm not sure if the helicopter being struck by lightning would have been a blessing or a curse.

While I was still airborne, my family was scrambling to get to Durham. My mom left our house in such a hurry to get to her baby boy that it wasn't until she reached the emergency room before she realized she was wearing bedroom slippers. Friends and family were gathered in the waiting room, hoping for any good news. After rushing with me to the helicopter, my mom and stepdad stumbled into the waiting room to pass on what they knew.

They were ready to hit the road, but also remembered all of their furniture was still sitting on the front porch and a suitcase needed to be packed. Mary Sutherland, the glass plant's lead nurse and the mother of one of my coworkers at the factory, was waiting with everyone else, and when she heard what was going on, she looked at my mom and said, "I'll take you." She later told me, "If that was my son, somebody would have stepped up for me. At that moment, I considered you my son. As a mother, I wouldn't want to be left behind."

On the way out to the car, a family friend saw my mom still wearing bedroom slippers, so she took her shoes off and swapped them with my mom before they hit the road. Once the trip started, Mary tried to get my mom's focus on anything other than my accident and what could potentially happen to me, a tough task for a two-hour drive. The only words Mary remembered my mom saying on numerous occasions was, "Are we okay?" She tried to assure my mom that they were, but neither was convinced.

While they were headed north toward Durham, my stepdad was headed south toward our house to pack a bag, move furniture inside, and make a very difficult phone call. As he pulled into the driveway, he saw the mountainous and monotonous job awaiting him. Furniture was everywhere except where it needed to be.

One task at a time. My stepdad, who is one of the most amazing men on the planet, dreaded making the phone call, but knew it had to be done. My sister, who lived three hours away, was working and this news would devastate her. He called, explained the situation to my sister's manager, and asked to speak to her.

I was trying to figure out how to express the thoughts and feelings of my sister when she first heard the news, but she's smarter than me, better looking than me, has more money than me, is more compassionate than me; the list could go on and on. Basically, all I got was the athleticism and humor. She got everything else. So I'm going to let her tell you in her own words.

But first, a little backstory about my sister and I. Her name is Christi, but as a kid, I called her "Sissy" because I was a rebel and did whatever I wanted (actually, that's just how I pronounced Christi, but whatever). She's nearly four years older than me, which greatly benefited both of us growing up. Once she started school, I had "class" many days after she hopped off the bus because she wanted to teach me what she learned that day. She must have been a great teacher—and still is as she's starting her 26th year teaching as of the writing of this book—because by the time I reached first grade, I was helping her with her fifth grade math homework (math never was nor ever will be her strong suit).

Her benefits, however, went far beyond honing her teaching skills. One day after school, one of her classmates beat me to our bus—Bus 96—so my usual seat next to her was occupied, so I sat across the aisle from him with her seated next to the window. Shortly after the bus departed, this boy started picking on my sister. Well, *nobody* picks on my sister (except for me, of course), so I told him to stop. He proceeded to hit her on the leg. From across the aisle, I punched him in the leg as hard as my little kindergarten fist could punch, followed with a warning: "Don't hit my sister!"

Whether he didn't heed my warning because of my size or because he had a crush on my sister was unclear to me, but he swung again, so I slugged him again and echoed my warning from earlier. When he raised his hand to throw a punch for the third time, I jumped out of my seat and my little fists of fury started flying. I still don't know how the fight ended. It's the only fight I've ever been in to this day (undefeated, baby!). I just remember the bus returning to school and sitting in the principal's office (the only time that ever happened, too). I was found guilty and sentenced to write 25 times, *I must not pass licks on bus 96.*

Now, that might seem like an easy punishment, but you need to realize, I was in kindergarten, still learning to write, and using a giant, foot-long pencil for whatever reason. It took me multiple hours and tears from a sore writing hand to finish, but my sister sat next to me and coached me through it until I was done.

That's a small snapshot of the relationship between my sister and I. We argued and squabbled with each other like 99 percent of siblings on the planet, but we had—and still have—each other's backs.

With that backdrop, here's my sister's story in her own words:

> It was a normal day at the Belk Estee Lauder counter when my manager called me into her office because she needed to speak to me. I was a little nervous because I thought I had done something wrong. When I reached her door, I was even more concerned by the expression on her face. She told me I had a phone call. My heart dropped into my stomach. I was trying to imagine who was dead.
>
> My stepdad was on the phone. I was in a full-blown panic now. He told me my brother had been in a bad accident and his arm was severed. I felt stunned. Severed???
>
> I remember asking him if severed meant cut off or just cut really badly. I knew what severed meant, but I just couldn't wrap my head around the idea of my brother losing his arm. My head was spinning. He told me Jeff was being airlifted to Duke. I told him I was going home to pack and was on my way.
>
> I started to cry and called one of my family members. He told me not to drive myself home because I was horribly upset, so my manager drove me home. The twenty-minute drive seemed to take an hour. I was replaying what my stepdad said over and over in my mind.
>
> I was still in college at the time, and I was taking a summer class. I decided on the drive home that I would quit the class I was taking because I didn't know what was going to happen to my brother. Nothing else seemed to matter.
>
> A family friend offered to fly me to Duke, but I told her I would drive. The trip seemed to take forever. I just

kept praying they could reattach his arm. I didn't think they could, but I was praying for a miracle.

When I arrived, Jeff was in surgery. The waiting room was packed with family and friends from my hometown. It was so comforting having them there. It was late, and we all spent the night in the waiting room. We were spread out on couches and chairs, while some were on the floor. We were talking, praying, crying, and, on and off, we were sleeping.

I remember the next morning, the waiting room attendant came in and seemed offended that we were there. It was as if we were bothering her and had made a mess of her space. I was so angry at her for seeming offended. She didn't ask why we were there or if we needed anything. She didn't know my 18-year-old brother only had one arm now. She didn't care, or, if she did, she didn't show it. I was so mad at her. I wondered how anyone could be so heartless.

Some of us went downstairs for breakfast. The hospital that had seemed to be asleep the night before was awake and lively. Elevators were opening and closing, people were talking, and doctors and nurses were hurrying around. I was mad about this, too. How could they be going on with their lives when my brother lost an arm in a stupid machine? I wanted them all to acknowledge his accident. I wanted them all to stop acting like life was normal. I wanted them all to look sad and concerned. I learned a hard life lesson that day — life goes on despite the burdens you are carrying.

The rest of the time at Duke seems to be a blur other than one incident. My stepdad pointed out something I hadn't noticed. One evening, my mom, my dad, and I were all around Jeff's bed tending to him. Even though my parents were divorced, our broken family didn't look broken. My stepdad, who loves my brother and me like his own, was happy that in the midst of a crisis, we were still united as one family. God was showing us that He was with us and revealing signs to us that everything was going to be okay; never the same, but Jeff was going to be okay.

CHAPTER 5

I Remember My Eyes Closing

By the time I arrived at Duke University Medical Center and was taken to the emergency room, I'd lost three-fourths of my blood. As a point of reference, think about a fuel gauge on a car. While everyone else was riding around with a full tank, mine was midway between a half tank and empty.

As I was waiting for surgery, I still had no information as to the condition of my right arm. I also didn't know the remains of my arm were in a cooler a few feet away from me. My hope remained that my arm could be reattached, and with some rehab, I'd get back to my life as normal with a sweet scar and a cool story.

Before any of my family arrived, my soon-to-be surgeon entered the emergency room. He told me he didn't believe reattaching my arm was an option, but the only way I know the words he spoke to or about me are from medical transcripts and legal documents. Here is his description of his first encounter with me:

> *"[Jeff] was conscious and appeared extremely scared. His arm had been severed and was on ice. He was emotionally in shock. He was alone. His parents had not arrived yet. I tried to take a medical history from him, but it was hard because he was extremely, you might say, catatonic. He couldn't. He was terrified."*

It's hard to describe the absolutely debilitating, gut-wrenching fear when you believe you could die at any moment. From the time I lost my arm at 1:40 p.m., I was terror-stricken. Fear suffocated me with each second that ticked away. I never knew when or if any single breath would be my last. I will tell you this though—you *never* want to live more than when you think you're dying.

By this point, I'd received a few hours worth of strong pain medication. A side effect of the medicine is drowsiness. The combination of meds, exhaustion, and perpetual fear finally caught up with me; I was out like a light.

When my mom reached Duke University Medical Center, she quickly found the ER and was escorted to my room. She didn't know if I was sedated or just asleep, but was glad I was resting. Either way, she wanted me to know she was there, so she came and prayed for me out-loud. She talked to me and told me she was there and would be with me until I went for surgery. She kept telling me I wasn't alone. Then, she walked over to the cooler and prayed over my arm and for wisdom for the doctors. She continued this process for over an hour, but she never stopped talking and praying because the mother inside her wanted to do everything in her power to let her son know he wasn't alone.

I wish I could say I heard her. I wish I knew she was there. I wish I heard her voice. I wish I heard her praying. But I didn't.

When I woke up, I was no longer in the ER. I'd been moved to the operating room during my slumber. I immediately noticed how bright, harsh, and metallic the OR looked. It felt like I was inside a UFO and the experiments were about to begin. Although medical staff were in the room with me, for the first time since my arm was ripped from my body, I felt completely alone...abandoned...lost.

I quickly realized I wouldn't be awake very long. They'd moved me to the OR because surgery was imminent. The staff buzzed all around me while I was strapped to a gurney, my left arm fastened around my bicep and wrist, my legs secured across my thighs.

As they administered the anesthesia, they told me to count backwards from 100. My fear spiked. I didn't want to go to sleep. My mind raced.

What if I never wake up? I don't want to die. I have to stay awake.

I tried sitting up, but my straps held firm. I struggled briefly, but knew my fate was sealed. Sleep was coming and there was absolutely nothing I could do about it. I laid back and started counting. I never reached 98.

I did not close my eyes. I actually fought against it, but I had no control in the situation. I vividly remember my eyes closing. I was terrified. I was scared they would never open again, and my last sight would be the ridiculously bright OR lights shining in my face.

My surgeon's doubts of replantation were confirmed once everything was literally laid out in front of him. I was on one table, my arm on another. It had traveled through 12 feet of the auger. My hand cleared the machine unscathed. The first sign of damage was three inches above the wrist joint, where the bone was crushed and the muscles cut.

They cleaned my arm—both the attached and unattached parts—extensively to clear any debris, mostly sand, captured from the job site. At this point, the surgeon had a, shall we say, *interesting* idea. He saw the remnants of my right arm still attached to my body and he saw a perfectly good right hand, but no salvageable forearm or elbow. He approached my family in the waiting room, told them a replantation of my arm was impossible, but a replantation of my hand was still an option. He believed he could attach my right hand to the end of my arm successfully.

To paint a pretty little picture for you, halfway between your shoulder and elbow where your right bicep is, I would have a right hand.

My parents asked a very logical question, "Will he be able to use it?"

"Probably not," was his response, "but it's never been done before."

Now I'm no brain surgeon, rocket scientist, brain scientist, or rocket surgeon, but I'm guessing there's a reason it's never been done before.

To paint another pretty little picture for you, halfway between your shoulder and elbow where your right bicep is, I would have a right hand...that didn't work.

Thankfully, my parents told him no, because if I woke up from surgery with my right hand attached to the end of my shortened arm, I would have been furious. I'd have wanted to punch somebody. If I was going to hit them with my newly attached right hand they would have to be standing *really* close when I swung. I mean, did he expect me to walk around clapping like a seal?

Don't get me wrong, I'm *very* thankful for everything he did for me that day and in the months to come. The surgery he performed (and the follow-up surgery) was nothing short of astounding. Because of the way my arm was torn from my body, I had more bone than skin remaining. Instead of doing extensive skin grafts on my body, he was able to use my "palmar filet flap to cover the humerus." In layman's terms, he cut the palm of my right hand and wrist off and used it to cover the remains of my upper arm. He was even able to connect an artery in my upper arm to an artery in my wrist to promote blood flow.

Although the surgery was a major success, that's not to say it wasn't without significant complications. Two times in the wee hours of the morning, my blood pressure plummeted. Throughout the surgery, the bottom number of my blood pressure stayed consistently around 60. Things began to go south, both literally and figuratively, around 3 a.m. when that number unexpectedly dropped into the 20s.

I was quickly given ephedrine, a stimulant which increases heart rate and blood pressure, in an effort to raise my BP. The medicine worked, as the bottom number climbed into the 60s again, but plummeted five minutes later back into the 20s. A second dose of ephedrine returned all of my levels to normal where they remained through the rest of my procedure.

I was in surgery for 11 hours and 13 minutes; my arm riddled with well over 100 stitches. While I lay prone in the OR, my mom, along with other friends and family members, was praying in the waiting room. She was praying my arm could be reattached, that I would be ok, and I would be able to live a normal life. She also prayed for others in the hospital who were in crisis (because that's just the kind of person my mom is).

But then she had just a flat-out moment of honesty with God, her prayer echoing the pain in her heart. "I tried to be a good mother and protect my children from harm when they were small. I wasn't there with Jeff when the accident happened, but You were. Why didn't You protect him?"

She heard an answer straight from Heaven that brought her peace even in the most dire circumstances as a mother. "I watched my Son die on the cross. That was for an eternal purpose. This too shall be for an eternal purpose."

It was then she remembered a verse God had given her three years earlier. May 19, 1990 to be exact. She was at a Christian women's event when God gave her a specific verse. She opened her Bible to Isaiah 8:18 (KJV). "Behold, I and the children whom the Lord hath given me are for signs and for wonders..." She didn't know exactly how at the time, but she knew God would use my accident somehow for His glory.

After I was taken into the recovery room, my parents were allowed to come see me. I was still heavily sedated and don't remember anything. My mom said the only noise I made during that time was when a member of the hospital staff made a painful mistake on my behalf.

I was laying flat on my back on the gurney. My right side and right arm were covered in blankets. The medical staff were trying to keep it as warm as possible to promote blood circulation. After a shift change, a nursing assistant entered my room. She saw a mound of blankets next to me, and being unfamiliar with my situation, decided to tidy up a bit.

She scooped up all the blankets, unaware my arm was included in her grasp. Even in my sedated state, I screamed in pain, which brought her attention to what she'd done. She made a comment along the lines of, "Oh, his arm was in there. Or what is left of it anyway." My mom, who is one of the most calm, non-confrontational people on the planet, issued a stern rebuke in her direction. (Never rouse a Mama Bear, even the non-confrontational ones.)

After four hours, I was moved to a regular room. It was here I remember waking up for the first time. I opened my eyes and my room was dark, save the light shining in from the hallway. I remember seeing a family friend standing in the doorway. She saw my eyes open and said, "Well there he is!"

Still extremely groggy, I rolled my head to the right to check the condition of my arm, hoping my surgeon's prediction was wrong and it would be reattached. It was still covered in blankets but I attempted to lift it. And that's the moment I knew it was gone.

I was frozen. Fear gripped me all over again. My gut wrenched, my heart sank, and my anger swelled. *How can this be happening? I freaking hate this! My life is over!*

Before anyone reached my bedside, I closed my eyes and went back to sleep. This time, however, I didn't care if they opened again.

CHAPTER 6

DARK DAYS AHEAD

[Author's note: This was the hardest chapter for me to write. It was also the hardest chapter of my life to live through and relive. But I want to make something abundantly clear. I'm not trying to make you, the reader, feel sorry for me in any way. I'm trying to tell you my state of mind during these darkest days of my life. The rest of the book won't be a pity party. Far from it, actually. The REALLY good stuff is in the pages and chapters still to come. But I am trying to paint the most accurate picture I can for you, no matter how dark it seems.]

I have no clue how long I slept. Nobody does. When you spend an extended period of time in the hospital, minutes bleed into hours, hours into days, and days into weeks. I do remember that each of the first few days, every time I woke up, I hoped the nightmare was over and my arm would be there. Whether it was from a nap or sleeping through the night, *every single time* I opened my eyes, I immediately looked at my right arm, praying the nightmare ended. Every single time I was met with another sucker punch to the gut of my new reality.

The next 16 days were hard. Very hard. During my surgery, I had a breathing tube inserted down my throat. Thankfully it was taken out before I woke up, but the sore throat it left behind made every swallow painful for days. The urinary catheter wasn't removed before I woke up, so that was tons of fun to have withdrawn. To top it off, I had an allergic reaction to one of the medications I was given to fight off infection, so my entire body broke out in a rash. Other than that and the fact I'd just lost my arm, was in constant pain, and depressed, everything was great!

I hated being in the hospital. I was constantly being poked and prodded by someone. I was always going from one appointment to another within the hospital. I had to be wheeled around to my appointments because, for the first few days, I couldn't even walk. The loss of my arm threw my balance off so I had to learn to walk again. I literally taught myself to walk by leaning my shoulder up against a wall and pushing myself down the hall.

And that wasn't the worst part. People stared at me everywhere I went. The remainder of my right arm was covered in a massive bandage. For a self-conscious 18 year old, it played the role of a neon arrow attached to me that read, "Please stare at the one-armed guy, no matter how much it seems to bother him" (it was a pretty big arrow).

Every day I was learning something new I couldn't do. Prior to my accident I was right handed. People look at me and say, "Now you're left handed," to which I reply, "Actually I'm only handed, but whatever."

The simplest of tasks were simply not so simple anymore. Transitioning from being a righty to a southpaw was very difficult and extremely frustrating. Things like getting dressed, tying my shoes, brushing my teeth, and eating required way more thought and effort than normal.

Speaking of eating, that was something I didn't do a lot of while I was hospitalized. The food wasn't great. How can I put this tactfully and delicately? It tasted like hot garbage. (Delicate enough?) I'd have rather chewed on my own foot than eat the food I was being served, but I'd already lost enough body parts at this point. I wasn't allowed regular food at the beginning of my stay, so I was served a healthy dose of chicken broth for most meals.

If you want the recipe for Duke University Medical Center's chicken broth, grab a pen and write this down so you can add it to your recipe book to impress any future dinner guests.

> *Step 1: Fill a cup with water.*
> *Step 2: Heat the cup of water in a microwave until lukewarm.*
> *Step 3: Remove cup from microwave.*
> *Step 4: Stir the water with a chicken leg.*
> *Step 5: Remove chicken leg.*
> *Step 6: Serve.*

Doesn't that sound delightful?

In my 16-day stay, I lost approximately 30 pounds. I entered the hospital at 158 pounds and left right around 130. It would have been more, but a week or so into my stay, a family member found a Domino's Pizza in the hospital, so I lived off of pepperoni pizza and breadsticks for the remainder of my hospitalization. (If losing my arm didn't kill me, I figured a lot of bread and grease couldn't take me out either.)

A bright spot to each and every day was when visitors showed up. It got pretty lonely and boring lying in a hospital bed all day, so there was nothing better than a knock at the door and seeing a familiar face walk in. And over the course of my stay, I saw more than a hundred people come through my door, quite a few of them making the two-hour drive multiple times to come see me. (For those of you who did who are reading this, I offer my sincerest thanks. You brought a little light to my darkest of days.)

My visitors not only brought some smiles, but also helped in the very beginning of my healing process. My doctors told my family not to mention the fact that I'd lost my arm until I brought it up. To this day, I'm still not sure of the rationale behind it, but they were adamant that no one talk about it until I did. And one day when a former high school baseball teammate was visiting, I told him, "I guess my baseball career is over because there aren't many one-armed Major Leaguers" (not that I had a chance anyway, unless a one-armed bat boy counts). Even though I'd been in the hospital for a few days, it was the first time I'd mentioned only having one arm.

That same teammate and future college roommate brought me a shirt that hung on the wall of my hospital room for the duration of my stay. In some ways, it became a reminder. In others, it became a challenge. It read:

absolutely
positively
most definitely
without a doubt
NO FEAR
(not even a little bit)

Walking out of the hospital after my 16-day stay was bittersweet. Sweet because I was going home; bitter because there were even more people to stare at me. In fairness, I understood why people stared. The bandage covering my arm was massive. It barely fit in my sleeve. I understood it, but I didn't like it.

Shortly after arriving home, my house turned into the go-to spot for Scotland High School's class of 1993 (or 19Naughty3 as our senior t-shirts read). Within an hour, the den in my house was full of my classmates. And by full, I mean F-U-L-L, full! Once the final guest arrived, there was nowhere left to sit. The couch where I was sitting was covered, including the armrests. Same with the two recliners, a rocking chair, our brick fireplace, and every square inch of carpet. There were more than 30 teenagers piled into a 216-square foot room.

It was a tight squeeze and my accident had caused a bit of claustrophobia on my behalf, but I loved every minute of having my friends there. I don't remember much about any particular conversations. I do remember there being a lot of laughter and little to no talk about my arm. It was refreshing to say the least.

Within a day or two of being home, I asked my mom if we could go to Quincy's to get a steak. When you live in a small town, the really nice steakhouses aren't an option, so Quincy's was our best spot. Their steaks weren't world famous, but by-God their yeast rolls were! My mouth is watering now just thinking about them.

When our server delivered our food, my stepdad prayed and we all dug in. Well, almost all of us. I stared at my steak. Not because I wasn't excited to see it, but because I didn't know how I was going to cut it. You see, when you cut a steak, you have a knife and a fork that work together as a team. Well, my team just got cut in half. So for me, it was either a knife *or* a fork. Using my lightning-quick deduction skills, I picked the knife because it's sharper.

I started sawing, but without a fork to keep the steak from moving, I was getting nowhere fast. I wanted to put my foot on it to keep it still, but that's just gross. It seemed like I chased the steak around the restaurant for 20 minutes. I've never been one to ask for help, so eventually I just gave up and started eating my fries.

My mom noticed I hadn't touched my steak and asked if something was wrong with it, to which I replied, "I don't know." She asked why I wasn't eating it and I told her I couldn't cut it. So an 18-year-old recent high school grad had to hand his plate across the table to his mom so she could cut his steak for him.

That's not embarrassing at all, wrote the author, dripping in sarcasm.

I know it doesn't seem like *that* big of a deal, but it was to me. I absolutely hated stuff like this. I just wanted to be able to do things for myself, especially things I was able to do before I got hurt. And the frustrating thing was, most of the time I was unaware of things I couldn't do (or that would take me *a lot* longer than normal) until I faced it in the moment. No time to prepare. No time to think up a solution in advance. Figuring things out on the spot when other people were around would make me break out in a cold sweat...literally. I didn't want to draw any attention to myself because I knew they'd see me standing there in all my one-armed glory and either stare at me or feel sorry for me. And I didn't want either. I just wanted to be normal, but normal was ripped from my grasp by that old, rusty screw auger.

One day for lunch, I stopped under the golden arches to grab some nuggets or a filet-o-fish (my go-tos at MickeyD's). Instead of zipping around the drive-thru, I decided on a whim to eat inside. After finishing up, I headed to the trash to dump my tray. Now remember, this was back in the day when there was a swinging wooden flap you had to push open to access the top of the trash can.

As I was walking toward it, I realized my predicament. In the past, I'd used one hand to push the flap open, and with the other, I'd dump my trash. That was no longer an option. I started sweating. So I slowed my pace and thought through my options.

One, I could ask for help. I quickly dismissed that idea because I didn't like asking for help, I didn't want to inconvenience anyone, and I knew that had the potential to make someone feel sorry for me.

Two, I could sit my tray on top of the trash can and push each individual item of trash in one at a time. I decided against that because it would take me much longer to do that and I didn't want to draw any extra attention to myself.

My third and final option was to try to push the flap open with the tray and dump it in one quick swoop. (Before I finish my trash can story, this was my thought process multiple times throughout a day unless I just stayed at home. I never knew when it was going to hit. Sometimes it still happens. It's exhausting. Utterly exhausting.) So, I forced the flap open with the tray when disaster struck. The flap slipped off the front of the tray and knocked everything onto the floor, including the tray, with a loud bang. I should have gone with option two. I cleaned up my mess as quickly as possible and got out of there.

I know you might be thinking *What's the big deal?* But things like that made me dread doing nearly anything because I never knew when a sneak attack was coming. Like eating at a buffet but there being no rails to put my plate on while I scooped my food. Or experiencing "phantom pain."

Phantom pain is pain that comes from a body part that is no longer there. I could be walking through Walmart, as if that wasn't painful enough, and my right elbow, forearm, hand, or a finger on that hand would start hurting. That was the only way I ever felt my non-existent right arm. And the pain ranged from annoying to excruciating and could last for a few seconds or a few hours. Sometimes it hit me in public and absolutely stopped me in my tracks, unable to move until the pain passed.

And to make matters worse, the timing of all these attacks—the trash can flaps, rail-less buffets, phantom pains—was terrible. I was 18, on the verge of my biggest step toward independence as my freshman year of college was fast approaching, and I could barely write my name as I was still learning to be a lefty. I'd soon be cutting ties from home, but needed help cutting my food. Things like that slapped me in the face and reminded me that life wasn't so simple anymore.

It wore on me and wore me down. I was frustrated beyond belief. I felt helpless and hopeless. I lived in a constant state of pain, anger, bitterness, and depression. Some nights I just cried myself to sleep because I was tired of it all.

CHAPTER 7

Parkway Drives

Before my accident, I'd been accepted to Appalachian State University in Boone, North Carolina. Most students choose their college based on their career path. I chose mine based on my friends' paths. At this point in my life, I had no clue what I wanted to be "when I grew up," but two of my closest friends—Steve Locklear, my fellow Pittsburgh Steelers fan since kindergarten and Keith Littlejohn, my brother from another mother since sixth grade—were headed to App. State so I became a Mountaineer too.

After my accident, my plans were delayed. Because of constant follow-up appointments to monitor the progress of my right arm and a scheduled revision surgery, I started my college career at Pembroke State University (now known as The University of North Carolina at Pembroke). Only 25 minutes from my parent's house, it was an easy commute and allowed a slow transition into college life. Mind you, I needed it as I plopped behind a college desk only 16 days removed from my hospital stay and one month after my accident. At this point, my handwriting could be described as *extremely* sketchy at best, and this was prior to the days of laptops, iPads, and iPhones, so typing wasn't an option. I'm one of the few people to start college without the ability to write.

I remember one of my first days in Freshman English we were given an in-class writing assignment. My heart sank and the cold sweat started. Not only was my penmanship terrible, it was excruciatingly slow. I don't remember the topic but I do remember the dread as I started writing. After roughly 10 minutes, I'd written two sentences; my neighbor, who happened to be one of my step-sisters, was completing her first page. *Fan-freaking-tastic.* To make matters worse, I made a mistake and needed to erase part of my assignment when I faced one of those sneak attacks I referenced in the last chapter.

How was I supposed to erase without having a second hand to hold the sheet of paper still? I started erasing as best I could when my paper split right down the middle. *Crap!* I sat and stared, gritting my teeth as my frustration surged. I was seconds away from walking out of class when I looked up at my professor. She'd been informed of my recent accident, as if the massive bandage adorning my right arm wasn't notice enough. She smiled at me and mouthed, "Don't worry about it. It's ok." I finished the assignment to the best of my ability, jumping the chasm that split the middle of my paper sometimes in the middle of a word.

Once my first semester, constant follow-up appointments, and another surgery were in the books, I transferred to ASU. By this time, I'd been fitted with a prosthetic arm. I didn't like it, but it filled the right sleeve on my long-sleeved shirts and the hand looked relatively real so I wore it in an attempt to appear normal. It didn't matter the temperature, I wore long sleeves. If it was 95 degrees, my sleeves were down to the wrist.

I was returning from class on a particularly hot day when a car full of people passed by. A guy yelled from his top-down convertible, "Hey! You know it's hot outside, right?" I wanted to scream at him, "Of course I do, you freaking idiot, but I'm extremely self conscious about having one arm!"

In my English class, my professor, who was unaware of my situation, actually made a boneheaded joke about how difficult it must be for people who lost an arm to have to wipe their butt with the opposite hand. Out of all of the things he could have said, he picked that one. Mortified and highly embarrassed, I slumped in my seat, pulled my hat down a little lower, and seethed through gritted teeth. Once the classroom emptied, we had an interesting exchange at the end of class, his facial expression changed immediately once I told him my story, followed quickly by an apology. I hated the constant reminders of what my life now was and it was nearly more than I could handle.

Little things like that just added to my anger, frustration, bitterness, and depression. When I walked around campus, I constantly kept my head down. I didn't have the confidence to hold my head up. In every one of my classes I sat in the desk closest to the door so I wouldn't have to walk in front of people. After a week or two of class, I knew everyone in class by the shoes they wore because I stared at the floor until class commenced.

And the worst part for me was looking in the mirror. I despised what I saw looking back at me. I usually slid to the right until I could no longer see the reflection of my arm. I had constant reminders on a daily basis. I didn't need the mirror staring at me too.

#TEACHABLEMOMENT
Do You Like What You See?

When I looked in the mirror, I hated what I was looking at. I hated the scars and the reminder of what I'd been through and that I didn't look "normal." The mirror was my enemy and a reminder of everything I wasn't.

That last paragraph more than likely "hit home" for a few of you readers. You hate what you see when you look in the mirror. It's probably not because you're missing an arm, but you might not like your nose, you might have acne, or there's a scar on your face. Or maybe, just maybe, your smile hides a scar from your life: a past transgression, a deep hurt you experienced at no fault of your own, a setback you're sure you'll never overcome. For you too, the mirror is your enemy and a reminder of everything you aren't.

I'm here to tell you that's not how it is supposed to be. Don't hate what you see when you look in the mirror, whether it's a visible or invisible scar, because the Bible tells us we were created in God's image (Gen. 1:27) and God doesn't make mistakes! We make mistakes, but God can heal us of those. Get in the Bible and find out who you are in Christ, because that is way more important than the reflection you see. No past pain, whether self-inflicted or inflicted upon you, can defeat you unless you allow it! I know. I've experienced it.

But in this season, I absolutely hated having one arm. I hated feeling handicapped. I hated my life. I walked around angry. I lived bitter, my jaw constantly clinched.

One night, I drove to an empty grocery store parking lot and had a shouting match with God. Well, I guess it wasn't really a shouting match because He never shouted back, but I sat in my black Chevy Blazer yelling and punching the steering wheel.

"WHY DID THIS HAVE TO HAPPEN TO ME?" I yelled into the darkness, tears cresting my cheeks, knuckles bruised and sore from repeated punches to the steering wheel. "WHAT DID I DO TO DESERVE THIS? ANSWER ME!"

You see, I thought God was responsible for my accident. I believed He caused it and I was being punished. I didn't understand and I demanded answers. Little did I know, the Bible says in John 10:10, "The thief does not come except to steal, and to kill, and to destroy. I (Jesus) have come that they may have life, and that they may have it more abundantly."

I was blaming God for something that wasn't His fault. That's the thing; He gets blamed for everything and gets credit for nothing. If something happens in your life that steals, kills, or destroys, *that's not God!* I wish I knew this verse that solitary night I was screaming in my car. But I didn't.

I'd yell and the silence echoed in return was deafening. My anger surged. There I sat alone in the dead of night...and I was done. I was absolutely done.

"God, You go Your way and I'll go mine. I'm done."

That was the last prayer I prayed for a long time.

Managing my freshman year four hours from home was difficult. I enjoyed the freedom and lack of supervision, but I missed the family support and having someone I could open up to face-to-face. My mom and stepdad were those people for me. One night I called home and my mom answered. I skipped the small talk.

"I want to come home."

Not for the weekend, but for good. And I meant it.

I was tired of it all. I started drinking quite a bit and not from peer pressure. I was hoping to dull the pain or get away from reality for a little while. It never helped. Nothing did.

"I just want to come home."

After a long talk, my mom convinced me to stay, even though I found out years later she wanted me home as well so she could "protect" me. I didn't want to be at college. I didn't want to be with my friends. At times, I didn't want to be anywhere.

On occasion, I'd take a drive on the Blue Ridge Parkway through the Appalachian Mountains because it wasn't far from the campus of App. St. But I wasn't always convinced I'd return. There were plenty of cliffs and overlooks lining the parkway. With tears pouring from my eyes, I contemplated veering my Blazer off the side of the road, ending it all. It would look like an accident.

I was tired of the overwhelming sadness. I was tired of bitterness eating away at my soul. I was tired of the crushing depression. I was tired. I wanted it all to end. But I just couldn't do it. I couldn't turn the wheel. Whether it was from fear or from knowing the pain it would cause my family or a combination of the two, my car's tires never left the pavement.

Looking back, I'm so thankful I didn't. Suicide is a permanent solution to a temporary problem. At the time, I didn't know the pain was temporary, but I would have missed a lot of amazing things in my life had I taken the easy way out.

CHAPTER 8

A Life-Changing Game of Pick-Up Basketball

With my college career at Appalachian State delayed a semester, by the time I arrived on campus, all of my high school buddies had already formed new friendships. So, by default, my number of friends spiked as soon as I made ASU my home.

My first college roommate was Allen Guinn, someone I'd played baseball with and against my entire life. Allen was just flat-out a good athlete. As a pitcher, he threw in the upper 80s; on the gridiron he was a quarterback, linebacker, and handled all of the kicking duties. His leg is what caught App. State's attention. He signed as a Mountaineer to boot kick-offs, punts, and long-distance field goals.

Having a football player as a roommate had some perks. Back then, all of the coaches on the sidelines wore headsets and none of them were wireless, so each coach had someone following him to keep his cord from getting tangled. After meeting Jerry Moore, Appalachian State's legendary head football coach, at a practice, I was given that awesome responsibility for him at all home games.

The funny thing is I wasn't very good at it. Actually, I was pretty terrible. For one, I *physically* wasn't capable of the job. You were supposed to hold the cable in one hand and wrap the excess with the other. I couldn't do that. So I held the cord in my only hand and a guy followed me who managed the excess. So I technically shadowed Coach wherever he went and never let go of the cord.

Also, I had no clue what I was doing. I'd never even been on the sidelines during a football game before, much less a collegiate game, and even much more less followed in the head coach's footsteps. Someone tried to give me some cord pointers before my first game, but how could he possibly remember to tell me *everything*? Like, I didn't know that if the play started coming my way, I was supposed to drop the cord so the players flying toward the bench wouldn't get caught in it. So the first time a play came our direction, Coach Moore stepped to the left, I stepped to the right, and the cord was hanging about waist high between us when our running back plowed through, snatching the cord out of my hand, and, more importantly, yanking the headset and hat completely off Coach's head, nearly pulling him to the ground, and breaking the headset in the process. Coach Moore, a devout Christian, just looked at me and asked for a new headset.

I wasn't sure why Coach kept me around until the Mountaineers finished their ninth game of the season. The team was 7-2, but they were 5-0 at home, including a huge 24-14 win over the number one ranked team in Division 1-AA at the time, the Marshall Thundering Herd. Remember, I didn't travel with the team, so I was only on the sidelines for home games. After ASU pulled off the narrowest of victories, a 41-40 win over Liberty University in the home confines of Kidd Brewer Stadium to notch their seventh victory, Coach Moore turned around with a smile on his face, smacked me upside the head with his play sheet and said, "You just might be our good luck charm!" (FYI, that lasted all of one game as we lost our last home game of the season in overtime against previously winless VMI and finished second in the conference standings.)

Being on the sideline during college football games was amazing, but the friendships formed with some of the players were even better. The thing I liked most was they never treated me like I was handicapped and they had my back no matter what, even if I did dominate them playing various sports games on the Super Nintendo. On a daily basis, someone, usually a football player, would enter our dorm room and challenge me to a game. The challenge was issued like this: "I want some of the chin music." I taught myself to play by using my left hand to control the directional pad while using my chin to press the buttons. Thus, "chin music" was born. And I was pretty good. At first I thought they were taking it easy on me, but once I got to know them better, I knew they would rather beat me and rub it in than lose to a one-armed guy. Those were the only sports

I could beat them at (I'd yet to get serious about golf) so I'd take what I could get.

They'd get me back in other areas. Like I said, they never treated me like I was handicapped, so whatever they were doing, they invited me along. I tried rock climbing with them once and briefly earned the nickname "Slide" after sliding down a rock and having another rock wedge slightly under my kneecap. That phrase, "If at first you don't succeed, try, try again" doesn't qualify for a one-armed guy attempting rock climbing. I was running out of body parts, so I let that potential hobby bypass me.

I did enjoy our time at the Quinn, ASU's recreation center, which boasted a weight room, racquetball courts, and four full-court basketball courts encircled by a track. We'd spend hours there playing basketball. I wasn't the best basketball player in the world, but I wasn't the worst either. I could hold my own if I didn't have to dribble a lot or shoot from long range (kind of the exact opposite of Steph Curry), so I spent most of my time playing defense and pulling rebounds.

One day when all of our classes were finished for the day, a group of us trekked up the hill to the Quinn to run a few games. Courts 1 and 2 were dissected by volleyball nets at half-court, so we ventured down to court 3 hoping to pick up a full-court game. There was already a group of guys there shooting around, so we joined in. Before long, captains were picked and teams started being chosen. Unfortunately, I didn't know either of the captains so I knew I'd go in the bottom of the draft (a.k.a. dead last). I understood because winners kept the court, so "the handicapped guy" might shorten their time on the court. I was always picked last unless one of my buddies was a captain.

That was my thought process until I counted to see how many players there were that day. Since we were going to play full court, we needed 10 players. We had 11. I knew that meant one person wasn't going to be picked.

Hmmmm, I wonder who that's going to be? Surely not the only one-armed guy on the court!

I looked around, hoping to see a guy there with no arms, but I had no such luck. So sure enough with the 10th pick, I wasn't selected. I scooped up an extra ball and walked over to court 2 to shoot by myself as my buddies assured me I'd have the next game on their court.

But this is where my story starts to make a major turn.

I vividly remember walking to the east end of court 2 and shooting by myself. I remember a half-court game being played on the opposite end, so I had this hoop all to myself.

The Quinn was busy that day, as it typically was when the weather turned for the better. October through March could be pretty rough in Boone, trudging to classes through snow, ice, and slush and literally walking uphill both ways (one of the benefits of attending college in the mountains). One night after an ill-advised walk to the campus grocery store in the snow and falling on my return voyage with bags of groceries in my hand, I flipped on the TV to find out the wind chill was 67 degrees below zero. Fun.

So when the weather made an upturn, the student body came out in full force. The Mall, a large field located in the center of campus, would be littered with people studying in the grass, guys throwing a frisbee, and numerous groups of tree huggers in a circle kicking around a Hacky Sack. The other hotspot was the Quinn.

As I mentioned earlier, the rec center had four basketball courts encompassed by a track with nets that hung between the courts and the track to keep the basketballs from tripping up the joggers and walkers. That day there was a steady flow as I shot hoops alone. I knew it wasn't an everyday occurrence to see a one-armed guy shooting basketball, so many of those on the track glanced at me and looked away before their brain had time to process what they just saw. More than 95 percent of them awarded me a second look, a great experience for a guy struggling mightily with self esteem. At least with college students it was typically a one-time thing. I'd get a second look and was usually ignored after that.

Except for one girl.

She looked at me, looked away, and then stared at me the rest of the time she walked by my court. Again, I understood it. I mean, it's a one-armed guy shooting basketball; not something you see every day. I didn't like it, but I understood it. But the next time she got to my court, she stared like I owed her money. I thought that was a little odd since she was a college student. The only people who normally stared at me that long were kids, and they'd usually say something to or about me very loudly to make it even better.

After her second pass, I figured she'd have gotten an eyeful and could go about her merry way. I was wrong. Each lap was paired with a stare-down as she passed by, and each time my level of aggravation grew. When people stared, it was another reminder to me that I didn't look "normal." I wanted to yell at her, "I'M NOT GOING TO DO ANY TRICKS! KEEP IT MOVING!" But I have a hard time being mean to people, even if they do something mean or aggravating to me.

After a few more laps, however, "the guy" in me started to kick in. My thoughts changed.

Wait a minute. Maybe she's "checking me out."

She wasn't, but I didn't know that at the time. A one-armed guy with zero self confidence doesn't randomly go introduce himself to a female (or at least this one-armed guy didn't). In fact, the entirety of my college years I asked *one* girl out on a date. It was a girl I shared a class with and we'd talked a few times. I summoned all, and I do mean all, of my courage to call her dorm room one day to ask her out, but she apologized and told me no, saying she had a boyfriend. She was so nice about it that, in hindsight, she probably was dating another guy, but my mindset at the time was so messed up that I just *knew* she turned me down because I only had one arm. I couldn't even bring myself to look at her the remainder of the semester and I definitely couldn't handle anymore rejection so I knew I'd be single for a long, long time.

That day at the Quinn Center, I thought my luck might change. It was extremely obvious that she was staring more than most people did, so I had to devise a plan to get her to come talk to me. There was a zero percent chance I would start the conversation. Z-E-R-O, zero! While shooting solitary jumpers on the east end of court 2, I did so from around the free-throw line. I decided to practice my shot from the baseline instead, that way if she mustered up the courage to talk to me, she'd have a shorter distance to travel because I'd be closer to the track.

My strategy worked to perfection as her first pass by my court after I'd moved to the baseline, she pushed the protective netting to the side and walked toward me. I wish I'd thought of something clever to say in case my plan succeeded, but I didn't. She initiated the conversation.

"Hi."

"Hey." (I was off to a good start.)

"How are you?"

"Good. How are you?" (Still solid.)

"Good. My name is Sheri."

"I'm Jeff. It's nice to meet you." (I said the right name, and I'm polite. Double win.)

The small talk continued for a while, but I knew she wanted to ask me a question. I wasn't sure what the question would be, but I knew a question was there. Would it be the question I was hoping for: would you like to go out with me? Or the question I dreaded: how'd you lose your arm? Or something completely different: how many chickens would it take to kill an elephant? (My best guess: seven.)

It ended up being none of the above. She asked me a much harder question.

"Would you like to go to church with me?"

Why couldn't she have just asked about my arm? No, I didn't want to go to church with her. Not at all. I was in a bad place with the Big Guy upstairs. I had no interest in going. The answer to this question would be easy.

"Sure." (Wait, what?)

She proceeded to tell me about the upcoming service, all the while my mind trying to figure out what the heck just happened. Yes, I was still very angry at God. Yes, I hated having one arm and thought He was the cause. But, there was a part of me that knew something was missing in my life, and not just my right arm. I didn't know it, but *something* was actually *Someone*.

CHAPTER 9

A Missionary From Africa

What do most college students find themselves doing on a Friday night? Visiting a new church by themselves to hear a missionary from Africa? No, just me? Well, that's exactly where I found myself.

I've never done great in crowds when I'm by myself. I was even worse after my accident. I've never been the guy who walks around and strikes up conversations. I usually stand against a wall and look for someone I know. After a while, if I don't find somebody, I leave. So when I walked into the crowded lobby of the church, which was a grocery store in its former life, I *really* wanted somebody to come talk to me. I felt as if I stood out like a sore thumb standing in the middle of the lobby, so I wandered over to a table in the corner adorned in a white linen cloth and started looking at the stacks of books and pamphlets. Occasionally I'd glance up as people entered the church, hoping I'd see someone I at least recognized. The chances of that happening were about as good as me giving someone a round of applause. It just wasn't going to happen. Each face that walked through the door was that of another stranger.

I was supposed to meet Sheri, but didn't know if she was already in the sanctuary or still on her way. I decided I'd wait in the lobby until service started. If I hadn't seen her by then, I was leaving.

Minutes, which seemed like hours, passed and I continued to stare at the table. I was really hoping someone—anyone—would strike up a conversation. A few times I took a quick look at a group of people gathered in a circle talking, but they were engrossed in their conversation. I was seriously ready to leave. I nearly had all the titles on the table memorized when, thankfully, Sheri walked in.

We walked into the sanctuary and found a couple of seats together. One of the first things that caught my eye upon entering the sanctuary was the various instruments on the platform. I was raised in a denominational church where we had a piano on one side of the choir loft and an organ on the other. Service always started with the organist behind the organ. The organist was also our pianist, so about halfway through the service, she would walk, typically barefooted, from the organ to the piano and finish the service out over there.

This renovated grocery store was completely different. The platform was home to numerous guitars, a keyboard, and a drum set. I was thinking *They must have had a concert here last night or something.* Imagine my surprise when the service started and I found out the instruments were actually a part of the church's praise and worship. Now, I didn't know it was called praise and worship. I called it the fast music and the slow music.

When the fast music started, most, if not all, of the college students around me started jumping up and down. I looked around like *What in the heck is going on here?* You would have thought House of Pain's "Jump Around" was being pumped through the sound system. I'd never seen anything like that in church before. And everybody around me was jumping. I didn't want to jump, but I wanted to at least seem like I was ok with it, so I started hopping, but my toes never left the floor.

When the fast music ended and the slow music began, a lot of people around me started to lift their hands. Again, I was confused because I'd never witnessed anything like that before. I was thinking to myself *I didn't even hear anybody ask a question but everybody around me seems to know the answer!* (Little did I know that they knew the Answer, and I was about to meet Him.) Again, not wanting to stick out, I half lifted my hand to where it was just below my shoulder, but was hoping nobody would call on me because I didn't even know the question, much less the answer.

After praise and worship was over, the minister took the stage. The speaker was a missionary in Africa, and he had been there a long time. I can't remember exactly how long, but it was roughly 487 years, give or take a couple of years. I'm pretty sure he invented Africa.

Anyway, as a reminder, I was still really upset with God because I blamed Him for taking my arm. So when the preaching started, I was very disinterested. He began his message by sharing some of the amazing things he'd seen God do on the mission field.

"I've seen blind eyes opened," he said with a smile on his face and passion in his voice.

All I was thinking was *I don't care.*

"I've seen deaf people able to hear again!" he exclaimed.

In my bitterness, my thoughts resonated *I don't care.*

"I've seen dead people raised to life again!"

An impressive claim, but I still didn't care. Why was God doing all of that for everybody else and He took my arm? *What else you got, Preacher Man?*

"I've seen arms grow out!"

You saw what now? That statement changed my thought process. I'm mad at God for taking my arm and he's watching God give them back. *Is there a sign-up sheet for that, Preach? Because I need two arms and nobody around here needs three!*

Needless to say, the preacher had captured my attention. I'd already decided I was getting my arm back by the end of service, and since it was a Friday and I didn't have class the following day, I was going to make the four-hour drive home, wake my mom and stepdad up, and show them my new arm.

After sharing some of the amazing miracles he'd seen on the mission field, the missionary started talking about the goodness of God. It was the first time in my life I'd heard anyone preach about John 10:10. That verse says, "The thief does not come except to steal, and to kill, and to destroy. I (Jesus) have come that they may have life, and that they may have it more abundantly." I realized the God he was talking about and the God I was mad at didn't line up. I was interested in the God he was preaching about.

#TEACHABLEMOMENT
God Didn't Take My Arm

If there is one thing I wish I'd known after my accident, it was the fact that God didn't take my arm. For the longest time I thought He had and it hindered me from wanting to get closer to Him. Once I did get closer to Him, that's when I really began to heal from all of the hurt I'd experienced. So me blaming Him delayed my healing.

All too often, God gets blamed for everything bad that takes place and gets no credit when something good happens. I just shared John 10:10 about how Jesus came to give us an abundant life, and it's the enemy (the devil) who steals, kills, and destroys. And Acts 10:38 says, "And you know that God anointed Jesus of Nazareth with the Holy Spirit and with power. Then Jesus went around doing good and *healing all who were oppressed* by the devil, for God was with him," (my emphasis in italics added). Notice it says "all who were oppressed by the devil," not "all who were oppressed by God."

Sickness doesn't come from God. He doesn't give people cancer to teach them a lesson. He doesn't kill people because He needed them in Heaven more than they were needed on Earth. If you've lost someone, it's not because God took them. It's because the enemy came to steal, kill, and destroy.

If you're mad at God because of something negative that happened to you, a friend, or a family member, your anger is misdirected. It was either an accident that happened due to human error or a sickness caused by the enemy. The sooner we are able to come to that understanding, the sooner we receive healing by drawing closer to God.

As he was wrapping up his message, the missionary asked the congregation a potentially life-changing question. I say "potentially" because the way we answered would make all the difference in the world (and for eternity). He asked, "Would you like to make Jesus the Lord and Savior of your life?"

Sheri, who was sitting next to me, leaned over and whispered, "Are you a Christian?"

"Yeah, I think so," I replied, unconvincingly. I was unconvinced for a few reasons. One, I was very angry at God when my shadow crossed the door of the church that night. The anger had subsided quite a bit after hearing the message, but I wasn't sure where that left me in God's eyes. Two, I wasn't sure what "made you" a Christian. If it was church attendance, then I should have been good. I was *always* in church as a kid. I often tell people I had a drug problem when I was growing up, because if the doors to our church were open, my mom *drug* me to church.

Sheri, as unconvinced with my answer as I was, whispered another question, "How do you know?"

Again, why couldn't she have just asked about my arm? I answered the best I knew how. "Well, I went to church my whole life. I even went three years in a row without missing a Sunday. I used to be the president of my church's youth group, and, before that, I was the vice president. I had speaking roles in church [translation: I was in the Christmas and Easter plays every year]. And I'm a good person."

The major component missing from my answer was Jesus.

Thankfully, she still wasn't convinced. "Would you like to go forward and pray with him just to be sure?"

I figured it wouldn't hurt, so I answered, "Sure," and the next thing I knew I was walking by myself to the front of the auditorium, probably near where the meat department would have been in the former grocery store, to pray with the missionary. There were roughly 15 others who accepted his invitation as well, and we lined up in front of the platform.

He told us about Jesus dying on the cross to save us from our sins, and how if we would confess with our mouths that Jesus is Lord and believe in our hearts that God raised Him from the dead, we would be saved (Romans 10:9). So that's exactly what we did as he led us through a prayer.

Now, let me tell you, that's not some magic formula that makes everything immediately better in your life, but for me, something changed. And it was instant. When I ventured down to the front of the sanctuary to pray with the missionary, it felt like I was carrying the weight of the world on my shoulders. But, remember, I was carrying a lot. I was weighed down with anxiety, fear, depression, worry, bitterness, suicidal thoughts, and self-hatred. But when I prayed and gave my life to Jesus, that changed. It was as if someone had removed a weighted vest from my body. That doesn't mean it's been smooth sailing for me ever since. I still have my issues, and I still have what I call my "one-armed days," which are days I feel particularly handicapped. But my life has been so much better since that night I gave my heart to Jesus.

And although people prayed for my arm that night, it wasn't healed. That miracle didn't happen. Was I a little disappointed? I'd be lying if I said I wasn't. But the disappointment was temporary. Very temporary. It was gone before I got in my car. Why? Something much more miraculous had taken place. For one, I just felt different. And I felt good. But, more importantly, my heart was changed. My life was changed. My calling was changed. My eternity was changed.

In that old grocery store, I didn't walk out carrying a lot of bags. I left my baggage inside.

CHAPTER 10

MY NEW FRIEND, RICK

After committing my life to Christ, I started attending a campus ministry at App. St. called New Life Ministries, a group that met every Monday night on campus. It was basically a weekly church service for college students held in a room of the student union. I was excited about the opportunity to grow in my knowledge of God and make some new friends along the way. In the beginning, one of those proved easier for me than the other.

I made a trip to a local Christian bookstore, bought a Bible, and started reading it every morning after my shower. When I first started, I tried reading before my shower, but had trouble staying awake, so I made a change that worked for me. I also wanted to make sure I had plenty of time to read, so I set my alarm 30 minutes earlier than normal every day. My roommate would still be sleeping, so I'd sit at my desk with my lamp on and start each day with some time with Jesus. It quickly became one of my favorite times of each day as I learned more about Him.

While I was growing in my faith, I couldn't say the same for growing my list of friends. I'd show up for service every Monday night, usually 10 to 15 minutes early, in the hopes of potentially making some new friends. I'd always sit in the back, because I still had some self-esteem issues. Week after week I would attend, and week after week I was never getting much more conversation than a nod or a "Hey" from someone as they walked by.

It reached a point after a couple of months that I had a phone conversation with my mom one Monday night before service.

Frustrated, I said, "If nobody talks to me tonight, I'm not going back."

I didn't want to lay down an ultimatum like that. I enjoyed learning more about God and being around people who shared my newfound faith, but I wished some of those people would just talk to me. Each service was like standing in the church lobby by myself that I talked about in the last chapter all over again. And the introvert and low self-esteem within me made it practically impossible for me to strike up a conversation. If somebody would initiate it, I could run with it. I just needed an initiator.

And, thank God, he showed up. His name was Rick Sizemore. He wasn't a student, but rather a leader of the campus ministry. I don't ever remember seeing him until that night, but I'll never forget him. He walked to the back row, slid in next to me, and started talking. I don't remember our exact conversation, but I remember he cared enough to sit down with a complete stranger and just talk.

One thing readily apparent about Rick was his love for people. After we talked that night, he walked me around the room and introduced me to people. I didn't remember everyone's name and they didn't always remember mine, but I never went to another service where I didn't have multiple conversations with the other students in attendance.

I noticed Rick doing that for others too. He was intentional about looking for people on the outskirts and doing his best to bring them into the group. He inspired me to get out of my shell a little bit more, so I started looking for people to reach out to as well. I'm not going to lie and say I did it every single service, but I became an extroverted introvert and at least tried.

And Rick did more than just introduce me to new people. He challenged me as I was growing in my faith, meeting with me regularly to talk about the Bible. Nearly each meeting started with the same question, "Who is Jeff Bardel?" As a baby Christian, I had no clue how to answer him.

It wasn't like Sunday School where nearly any question could be answered with "Jesus!" and you'd be right more often than not. I'd try different answers every time, hoping that eventually I'd get it right.

"A Christian," was one reply. "A son," was another. "A student," was yet another.

Rick would usually smile and ask one of two follow-up questions; "What else?" or "How do you know?"

"You tell me," was my go-to if my first response wasn't satisfactory. And I was neither smart enough nor capable of writing a correct answer on my hand before we met, you know, because of me only having one arm and all.

But Rick (and his frustrating question) was trying to get me to change my thought process. He wanted me to see myself the way God sees me. I began to learn some good answers to his question:

- A new creation (2 Corinthians 5:17)
- Not condemned (Romans 8:1)
- Right with God (2 Corinthians 5:21)
- A conqueror (Romans 8:37)

Rick played such a key role in pushing me forward in my knowledge of God. He explained verses I didn't understand and was always available to answer any of my questions. Little did I know that within a few months, one question he would ask would change the course of my life forever.

CHAPTER 11

"Will You Share Your Testimony Tonight?"

It was a normal Monday night for me. My classes done for the day, I was hanging out in the student union waiting for New Life's Monday night service to start. I'd been saved less than a year, but I was growing in my faith. My morning Bible reading was still a regular part of my day, and I practically never missed a Sunday morning or Monday evening service.

I was also trying to get more involved, stepping out of my comfort zone a little bit at a time. So when Rick brought up a chance to be a youth leader at a weekend youth retreat called Novemberumba, I immediately jumped at the opportunity. I didn't even know what all I'd be doing, but I knew I wanted to be there.

Or at least I *thought* I wanted to be there. That's when the enemy started attacking.

Now, let me hit the pause button here and explain something to you. I'm not one of those people that believes that anytime anything bad happens, the devil is out to get me. I do know the enemy does fight against us, sometimes stronger than others. But I also know that sometimes bad things happen in life because people make stupid decisions. Take, for instance, my accident. Somebody made the stupid decision to take all of the safety equipment off of the screw auger. As a naive 18 year old, I made the stupid decision to put my hand inside the auger. The devil didn't grab my arm and force it into the machine.

On the other hand, I do believe we have an enemy out there whose job it is to steal, kill, and destroy (John 10:10). And I believe another thing the enemy does is plant doubt. The very first question in the Bible came from Satan as he was trying to make Adam and Eve doubt what God spoke to them (Genesis 3:1–4). And in John 8:44, Jesus calls the devil "the father of lies."

I believe that's what happened to me when I knew I was supposed to be a youth leader at this retreat. I kept thinking things like *You don't know the Bible well enough. You can't quote the Bible from the Table of Contents to the Book of Maps. You still don't understand everything that you read.* I started doubting whether I was supposed to go because how could I possibly help anyone.

I'd already told Rick that I'd go, but now I had to come up with a good excuse for why I wouldn't be there. It didn't take me long to come up with one. The weekend of the event coincided with the last career football game for one of my best buddies on the football team. I couldn't possibly miss that! And that's what I was going to tell Rick.

Or, at least that's what I *thought* I was going to tell him.

No sooner had I come up with that excuse when God nudged me and said, "Jeff, you know he's not going to play." And it was true. I knew he wasn't going to get in the game. In fact, in his four-year career playing in the black and gold of Appalachian State, he played in a total of five games. In those five contests, he mainly played special teams and notched one more tackle than I did in my four-year career of watching from the stands. So I knew in good conscience I couldn't tell Rick that was my reason for not going, so I came up with another plan. I would go, but I would plaster myself against a wall and just watch. I wouldn't get involved at all. I felt like that was a solid plan, but I didn't know Rick had one more question up his sleeve.

So, in November 1996, a group of 10 students from App. State made the hour and a half trip from Boone to Ridgecrest, North Carolina, to the Ridgecrest Conference Center, located in the Blue Ridge Mountains. Everyone was excited to impact the lives of the youth in attendance. Well, almost everyone. I was excited to watch from the sidelines as my friends impacted the lives of the youth in attendance.

On the first day, my plan went off without a hitch as I literally leaned my prosthetic arm against a wall and watched as everyone else mingled, talked, and even prayed with the kids who were there. It was pretty cool to be able to watch as God moved in the lives of those youth, but I was comfortable where I stood.

On day two, Rick pulled our squad together for a team meeting. He discussed things from the day before that he really liked and some areas he'd like to see us improve in; things like get involved with the kids and don't stand off to the side. Basically what he was telling "us" to do was not do what I had done on day one. But Rick did everything from a heart of love, so he never called me by name, but I heard him loud and clear. Just when I thought the meeting was ending, Rick looked at me and asked a question that is still impacting my life to this very day and it will until I enter the Pearly Gates.

"Hey, Jeff, will you share your testimony tonight?"

I loved Rick so much, almost anything he would ask me to do, I'd do because I knew he had my best interest in mind. So my response was, "I sure will." And then I added a question of my own. "But what's a testimony?"

Before you think I'm a complete idiot, I knew what a testimony was in a court of law. I actually had to testify before the industrial commission after my accident, so I knew what that kind of testimony was, but I wasn't sure about a church version. Rick got a good laugh at that and told me to just talk about what Jesus had done in my life up to that point.

"Got it! No problem!"

I'm sure he gave me a time limit, but I'm also sure I didn't need it. When I told Rick, "Got it! No problem," that's the only lie I ever told that man. And it was a flat-out lie! Public speaking terrified me. As a Communications major, Public Speaking was a required course of mine. I remember my first day of class, I wasn't too worried because our professor was just going over the syllabus with us. Then disaster struck!

About halfway through the syllabus, he stopped, apologized, and said he meant to tell us something when class first started but it slipped his mind. His announcement:

EVERYONE OF YOU WILL GIVE A TWO-MINUTE SPEECH TODAY ABOUT WHAT MAKES YOU DIFFERENT FROM EVERYONE ELSE IN THE CLASS!!!!!!!

Ok, he didn't shout it and the seven exclamation points might be a slight exaggeration, but that's how I heard it. And then he just resumed going over the syllabus, oblivious to the fact that he just nuked my very soul with his announcement.

I have a nervous "tell" that is very apparent when I'm sitting down. I start moving my legs back and forth, away from each other and then toward each other. The more nervous I am, the faster my legs move. That day in Public Speaking my legs looked like hummingbird wings. I'm surprised I didn't fly around the classroom screaming, "I don't want to give a speech today! What kind of class does he think this is?"

Um, Jeff, it is a public speaking class.

There were only 20 of us signed up for that course. Thankfully we didn't go in alphabetical order, because "Bardel" would have been first or second I'm sure. Instead, whenever you were ready, you walked to the podium and gave your speech. As more and more of my classmates knocked out their speeches, I became more and more nervous. There's no telling how many calories I burned as my legs flailed violently underneath my desk, but my pants fit a little looser when I walked out of class that day.

Speeches continued for nearly 40 minutes, and then a noticeable lull. The professor, who was sitting a couple of desks directly behind me, announced that there were only two students remaining. It just so happened to be me and the guy sitting next to me. He glanced at me and asked, "Do you want to go?" If he meant, "Do you want to go (grab a pizza)?" I would have answered, "Heck yes! Hawaiian or buffalo chicken please!" If he meant, "Do you want to go (out of this classroom and never come back)?" Again, I would have answered in the affirmative. Even if he meant, "Do you want to go? Do you want to fight?" I probably would have said yes if it meant I didn't have to give a speech that day. But I knew what he meant. I shook my head.

After my neighbor finished his speech, I walked on trembling legs to the podium. At this point in my life, thanks to Jesus, I'd become a little more confident and only wore my prosthetic when it was cold. This was the first day of class in September so the weather was still warm. As I parked myself behind the podium, an inch of sock-covered arm poking out of my green Polo sleeve, I started my speech.

"My name is Jeff Bardel, and it didn't take me very long to figure out how I'm different from all of you." I capped that with a slight nod to my missing right arm. Half of the class laughed; the rest smiled nervously. I vaguely remember telling the class how I lost my arm.

But there are two things I easily recall about that day. One girl in the class said she was different because she'd never met anyone who, like her, could snap their fingers using their thumb and pinky. She demonstrated with a loud snap. It wasn't all that impressive until each of us tried and failed. (You probably just did too.) The second thing I remember is how much more comfortable I felt walking into class knowing I didn't have to hide my missing arm, something I'd become an expert at in three years. To nail it down, the next speech I gave was entitled, "The Challenges of One-Armed Living," and I even included the story from earlier in this book when I nearly got the head football coach decapitated.

That paints a little backstory for you on who exactly Rick had asked to share his testimony in front of 200 youth that night. I stood in the back of the room battling a crippling headache, no doubt because of my nerves, as service started. I was standing so my "tell" wasn't as obvious, but I was swaying back and forth pretty hard. Thankfully, praise and worship was happening at the time, so it just looked like I was moving with the music. Once it ended, Rick grabbed the mic and called me up front as he started introducing me. That was both the longest and shortest walk of my life.

When I finally arrived at my destination, I had no idea what I was going to say. My mind was blank as Rick handed me the mic. In a matter of seconds, he retrieved it as he noticed how bad my hand was shaking. Ray Charles and Stevie Wonder would have noticed how bad it was shaking. I'm convinced I'd have given myself a black eye if the mic stayed in my hand.

To be honest, it was fitting the way it all worked out because Rick stood by my side, as he had for the majority of my Christian walk, and held the mic for me as I started talking. To this day, I have absolutely zero recollection of what I said. I'm guessing I talked about how I lost my arm, but, for all I know, I could have talked about monkeys riding roller coasters. (I doubt that's what I talked about as I have limited knowledge of the subject.)

I do remember Rick talking once I was finished. He put his arm around my shoulder and said something along the lines of, "You've just heard what Jesus did in Jeff's life. He can do the same thing in yours. If you'd like to accept Jesus as your Lord and Savior, get out of your seat and come up to the front so we can pray with you."

I was thinking *We? Who said anything about me praying? Rick will pray and I will agree with whatever he says.*

There were 400+ eyes staring at us as we waited and watched. Without any more prodding or pleading, one 13-year-old boy, who was sitting in the back left corner of the auditorium, rose from his seat, walked down front, and stood directly in front of Rick and I with tears in his eyes. He wanted to give his life to Jesus! I listened as Rick talked with him, and eventually prayed with him to make Jesus the Lord of his life. (I fulfilled my role. I stood next to Rick and agreed with what he said. #NailedIt)

I was blown away that God allowed me to be a part of that. He had used my accident to bring someone to Him! My test had become a testimony. From tragedy came triumph.

In that moment I whispered a simple prayer. It wasn't anything eloquent. I'd never heard anybody pray a prayer that was even slightly similar. Centuries from now, scholars won't write dissertations about the words I said. But it was spoken out of a pure heart with even purer intentions.

"God, that was really cool. If You want me to do that again, I will."

That's the thing about prayer. I feel like we complicate it too much. Just talk to God about what's on your heart. No need to be fancy. No need to use King James English—"Dearest Father of Lights who doth rainith on high in the clouds of glory." No, just say, "Dear God," or "Hey God," or however you would talk to a friend.

And He answered that simple prayer, and He continues to answer that simple prayer to this very day. He started giving me more opportunities. The next time I shared my story, lives were changed. Not only those in attendance but mine as well. God dropped a bomb on me that shook me to my core. It continues to shake me to my core to this very day. And it just might shake you to yours as well.

CHAPTER 12

"IF YOU WOULD HAVE DIED THAT DAY..."

Less than five months later, I found myself standing behind a mic in front of a crowd of more than 700 people. My eyes were still red and my nose a little runny because I bawled my eyes out mere minutes before taking the stage. And no, it wasn't because of the size of the crowd. The sizes of my audiences had gotten progressively larger; from 20 in my Public Speaking class, to 200 at Novemberumba, to now 700, but I had been crying for an entirely different reason. But let's not get ahead of ourselves.

The year was 1997 and I was wrapping up my junior year of college at Appalachian State. I'd developed some really close friendships with some incoming freshman that year, two in particular being Summer Harpold and Angela Rogers. I'd seen them around campus, at church, and at New Life services, but I got to know them sitting in a booth by the window inside Mel's Diner, a 1950s-style eatery with good burgers and amazing milkshakes. But we weren't there to eat. We weren't there on a date. We were there to meet a band.

No, we weren't groupies. I'd never even heard of the band, but I seemed to be the only one in Mel's Diner that night who'd never heard of them. They were the Christian rock band, *Third Day*. Everybody was making a big deal out of potentially meeting them so I tagged along, but mostly just to hang out.

It looked like a New Life takeover of Mel's, as we packed the place out around 11 p.m. I found myself in a crowded booth smashed up against the window, sitting across from Summer and Angela. Summer was a freckle-faced, ringlet-blonde with a big smile and infectious laugh. If Summer was awake, she was smiling. Angela was vertically-challenged, standing at a whopping 5', with a country accent, a love for music, and a smile for days.

We sat in that booth and waited and talked.
And waited and talked.
And waited and talked.

When 2 a.m. rolled around, there was still no sign of *Third Day*, so everybody decided to head home, but I'd made some awesome new friends, so it was worth the wait.

A lot like myself, Summer and Angela were very faithful to show up to services, 7 a.m. prayer meetings, and anything else New Life hosted, so we started hanging out on practically a daily basis. Spending that much time together, you began to learn each other's stories.

They were both raised in Christian homes, and I was convinced Summer had never sinned. She was optimistically optimistic and saw the best in everyone. Angela had battled depression and an eating disorder, but came out shining like Jesus on the other side.

All three of us developed hearts for ministry and wanted to help out people any way that we could. We even started a hospital ministry while at Appalachian State. The thought came from the time I spent in the hospital after my accident. On days when I had few or no visitors, it got extremely lonely. So, with permission from the hospital, we would visit and pray with patients, as well as leave Bibles behind for them to read if they didn't own one.

There was one gentleman in particular who really pulled on our heartstrings. He was in his mid- to late 80s and recently lost his elderly wife. He had no family on the East Coast, so he was alone in the hospital unless a doctor or nurse visited his room. As we were walking the hallways of the hospital, we prayed for God to lead us to the right rooms. As I walked by this gentleman's room, he said in a loud voice, "Somebody please come in here and talk to me!"

I thought to myself *That's either an answer to prayer or a willing audience!* (We had definitely encountered some unwilling people, so we honored their requests and left them alone, even though some continued yelling as we walked away.) We entered the room and my heart broke. He didn't appear to be doing very well and was in the room all by himself. During my hospital stay, I was never alone, as a family member was with me 24 hours a day except when hospital staff cleared my room for blood draws or my catheter extraction.

That day, we visited his room for more than 30 minutes, learning about his life and family. Before we left, we prayed with him and gave him a Bible. He started crying and thanked us profusely. As we were ready to leave, he asked, "Will you please come visit me again?" We promised we would and visited him again before the week was over. As we were leaving the second time, he again asked, "Will you please come visit me again?" I assured him that I would, even if I had to come by myself.

The beginning of the following week, we piled in my Blazer and drove back to the Watauga Medical Center. When we arrived at his room, I knocked on the door as we entered. To my surprise, the room was empty. None of his effects were there; not even a "Get Well" card on the bedside table. Confused, I hurried to the nurses station and inquired about the gentleman we'd grown to love. The nurse behind the desk answered stoically, "He is no longer with us."

I stood there in disbelief as my eyes filled with tears. The nurse saw my reaction and clarified very quickly, "No, no, no! He didn't pass away! He made a dramatic recovery and was able to go home." I was both relieved and sad at the same time. I was thankful his health had improved to that extent, but was sad I'd not be able to visit with him anymore (the hospital wasn't allowed to give us his personal information as we weren't family).

It was encounters like that where we were able to share the love of Jesus that we lived for. With that in mind, Angela invited me to her hometown of Taylorsville, North Carolina, to speak at an event called One Way, an idea God gave her as an outreach to her county. I'd never been there, and the first time I heard of it was when Angela, who we lovingly referred to as "Boog," told me that's where she was from. Taylorsville, located an hour north of Charlotte, boasted a population of 2,241 people in 1997, which makes the 700 in attendance all the more astounding. That means nearly one out of every three people in Taylorsville showed up!

Alexander Central High School was the home for One Way '97. There were a few speakers on the docket, as well as two local Christian bands. The speakers were Clayton King, one of the most dynamic preachers I've ever heard, as well as former Duke basketball player Robert Brickey, and myself. You know Jesus had to be involved if me, a Tar Heel, could preach at the same event as Brickey, a former Blue Devil. The two bands were *Mercy Seat* and Clayton's band, *Monogamous Fish*.

The event was on a Friday night, so after our classes ended for the day, we made the hour-long drive to Taylorsville to help set up for the event. When we showed up at ACHS, the gym was barren except for the bleachers lining the basketball court and a few volunteers who were beginning to set up. We hit the ground running and started setting up folding chairs in two sections across the gym floor with an aisle down the middle. We were about four rows deep when one of the volunteers walked up and asked me a question.

"Aren't you one of the speakers tonight?"

"Yes ma'am."

"What are you going to talk about?"

And that's when it hit me. I hadn't prepared anything. I didn't have a Bible verse picked out. I didn't have a topic. I don't know if it just slipped my mind or what, but I had nothing. Absolutely nothing.

I don't remember how I answered her because, at that moment, I was freaking out. I started looking for Summer or Angela. I didn't want to ask them to pray for me or what they thought I should speak about; I wanted to ask them if I could borrow their Bible. Why, you might ask? Yep, you guessed it! The preacher had left his Bible at home! I swear I'd lose my right arm if it wasn't attached to my body. (Oh, wait...)

I spotted Summer across the gym, hurried over to her, and explained my predicament. She grabbed her Bible (remember, Summer *never* sinned and *always* had her Bible) and extended it to me. I glanced at it and chuckled. It was pink. Oh man, did I have jokes. But what I didn't have was time (or my Bible), so I took it and looked for a quiet place to sit. The gym was too noisy with all of the setup going on, so I walked outside and saw a picnic table in the distance. It seemed secluded enough to get away from the noise and people who might distract me, so I jogged out and sat down. I opened the Bible, closed my eyes, and prayed.

"Lord, I'm sorry I haven't prepared anything. I don't know what I was thinking. Please speak to me. I need to hear from You. What do You want me to talk about tonight?"

I frantically flipped the pages of the Bible back and forth, trying to find something to preach about. The only thing moving more frantically than the pages were my legs, as they were going a mile a minute under that picnic table, much like they were that first day of my Public Speaking class. I'd read a passage, and then go find another one. I wasn't getting anything.

There was a slight breeze that day, so I draped my arm over the edge of the left page to keep the pages from turning. Frustrated, I put my hand over my eyes and, again, asked the Lord to speak to me. When I removed the blindfold of my left hand, I saw the pages of the Bible were flipping as the breeze strengthened. I just sat and watched them, frustrated with myself for not preparing anything prior to coming.

As I sat there, something strange happened. The wind continued to blow, but the pages of the Bible stopped flipping. It stopped on Job 32.

"God, do You want me to preach on Job 32? I've never read it (I spent the majority of my time reading the New Testament), but if You want me to, I will."

I didn't hear anything, so I started reading. I read through the first 17 verses and barely understood anything I read. But then I reached verses 18, 19, and 20 and they jumped off the page at me.

Job 32:18–20

18 For I am full of words;
The spirit within me compels me.
19 Indeed my belly is like wine that has no vent;
It is ready to burst like new wineskins.
20 I will speak, that I may find relief;
I must open my lips and answer.

I couldn't believe what I was reading. It seemed like God sat down at that picnic table and told me, "Don't worry about what you're going to say. The words are already inside you and My Spirit will tell you what to say." I still didn't know what I was going to say, but I knew I'd have something by the time I got behind the mic.

#TEACHABLEMOMENT
Ways God Speaks

I've been in conversations with people before and mentioned when God spoke something to me, and they responded, "Wait, God talked to you?" Like it was something weird or unheard of. So I wanted to share a little bit on this subject.

There are many different ways God can and will speak to you. First and foremost though is through the Bible. That is God talking to you, especially the New Testament because of what Jesus did for us on the cross. That's why you hear a lot of pastors and preachers talk about the importance of reading your Bible. That is the primary way we will hear from Him.

I've had a few instances of God speaking to me in other ways, which you'll read later in this book. There's also another #TeachableMoment about people who "always hear from God" you'll want to read.

I believe God led me to that passage in Job for a specific reason in this specific instance. I don't typically read my Bible outside and wait for the wind to blow the pages and read wherever it stops. That would be silly.

I'm also not a fan of opening the Bible, closing my eyes, pointing to a verse, and thinking that's exactly what God wanted me to read. Have I done that in the past? Yes, when I was a young Christian that didn't know the Holy Spirit very well. I had been invited on a mission trip to Macedonia and was seeking direction. I asked God to give me guidance through His Word and I opened directly to a passage in Acts 16:9 that said, "And a vision appeared to Paul in the night. A man of Macedonia stood and pleaded with him, saying, 'Come over to Macedonia and help us.'" Well, I had my direction! But, as I've grown in my relationship with God, I

> don't need to be led that way any more. That was nice, but I can't always rely on His direction to come that way. If I'm trying to decide to buy a certain car, I can't open the Bible and expect it to say, "Buy that blue Jeep Rubicon with black wheels and a black hardtop." (Now, if God tells you to do that for me, be led! Haha!)
>
> But I trust my ability to know what God wants me to do in various situations, and ask Him to correct my path if I missed Him. The more you know God and His Word, the easier it is to hear His voice and not be fooled by the voice of the enemy.
>
> Jesus said it best, as He always does, "My sheep hear My voice, and I know them, and they follow Me," (John 10:27).

Feeling much more at ease, I ran back to the gym and resumed setting up chairs. I still didn't know what I was going to talk about, but I knew it was going to be good. I just had no clue how much it would shock me.

Within a few hours, setup was complete, and busloads of people started showing up. Before long, the chairs and bleachers were full, and service was ready to start. I was seated in the front row in the fourth seat from the center aisle. Summer was seated to my left, Angela to my right. A wooden podium sat center-stage. On the floor directly in front of me near the stage stood a small table holding seven candles standing at attention. As the service began, a youth pastor from the area solemnly walked toward the table, lighter in hand, setting each candle ablaze.

Clueless as to what was going on, I leaned over to Angela and asked why the candles were being lit and why there were so many. She told me that in the last six months, seven teenagers in

Taylorsville had died from car accidents or suicide. The candles were lit as a memorial for them.

When I heard those words, I started crying. And that was very unusual for me, because growing up, I didn't cry often. There are only a few instances I remember although I know there were more. When I was five or six years old, my Papa bought me a birthday present. It was a baseball bat, glove, and a baseball, but it wasn't in a box. It was just wrapped in wrapping paper. I guessed what it was just by looking at it. Later that night, my mom walked in my bedroom and found me crying in my bed. She asked me what was wrong, and I told her I thought I hurt my Papa's feelings by guessing his gift for me. It literally bothered me for years! An extra-inning loss on the diamond when I played for McDonald's in Little League forced me to tears, but a hot fudge sundae from the team I represented dried those up pretty quickly. In the fourth grade, I cried when my parents sat my sister and I down to tell us they were separating. I didn't know what that meant, but my eighth-grade sister was crying so I knew it must have been bad. About a year later, our calico cat, Prissy, who was a neighborhood cat that my sister and I fed secretly until she claimed us as her family, died. A few years later, our solid black Dachshund, Tina, who had been a part of our family for all 13 years of my life, passed away. Both of their deaths made me bawl like a baby, even though I never wanted to cry in front of my mom or sister after my dad left because I was now the "man of the house." But the soft spot in my heart for animals overwhelmed me each of those nights. Other than those times in my life, tears never came easily. In fact, the first time I cried after I lost my arm was five days into my hospital stay, and it wasn't because of the pain. It was because my baseball career was officially over.

So when tears started rolling down my cheeks that night, it surprised me. *Why am I crying?* I thought. *I didn't know any of these kids.* Any time somebody dies it's sad, but especially when it's a young person, because they never really had a shot at life. I figured that's why I was crying.

I figured wrong.

Before long, I went from crying to sobbing uncontrollably. I was an absolute mess. I was sitting with my left arm folded across my chest, left hand clutching my right shoulder, my head between my knees, bawling my eyes out. I was thankful Robert Brickey was speaking first, because I was useless when it was time for the first speaker. As he took the stage, I sat on the front row openly weeping. Everyone within arm's reach of me had their hands on me praying and their words were probably something like, "Lord, you better calm this one-armed white boy down because he is supposed to speak in a few minutes."

And here is where my life, my testimony, and my calling made a major shift.

Even though I was still relatively young in my faith, I knew God was dealing with me about something. So, with tears pouring down my cheeks, I prayed a really deep, spiritual prayer the likes that no one outside the Bible could have ever brought before God. I'm pretty sure it's in the Bible somewhere, probably something the Apostle Paul, Moses, Peter, or even Jesus Himself prayed.

My prayer was, "God, what's up?" (That's deep, right? Like I said, I'm pretty sure it's in the Bible. It's either in 1 Hesitations or 2 Reservations. But, like I wrote earlier, God doesn't need formality in prayer. He just wants to talk.)

When I asked that question, God answered me. He reminded me that after my accident, I always asked Him, "Why me?" And I did. All the time. My conversations with God would go something like this, "God, why did it have to be me? Why couldn't it have been so-and-so?" And then I would list the reasons why "so-and-so" was more qualified to lose an arm than I was. There were a few so-and-so's I asked about regularly. I was just voicing my frustrations because I knew God wasn't going to turn back the clock and right my wrong. With tears still falling from my eyes, God continued our conversation.

"You never asked Me why I let you live that day."

"Okay, God, why did You let me live that day?," I prayed quietly to myself. "Why didn't I just die and go to Heaven to be with You?"

The answer I heard in reply was audible. It was a masculine voice. It startled me because I heard it with my ears, not spoken to my spirit like He had spoken to me just seconds before. It was so loud I asked both Summer and Angela, "Did you hear that?" Neither of them heard anything. No one around me did. God had literally just spoken to me. And His answer scared me.

"If you would have died that day, you would have gone to Hell."

(Read that again.)

(One more time.)

(Now think about it.)

I was on my way to Hell, and I had no idea! If I didn't survive my accident, I'd be burning in Hell right now.

#TEACHABLEMOMENT
How Can a Loving God Send People to Hell?

I've heard people ask the question, "How can a loving God send people to Hell?" My answer: He doesn't. God doesn't send anybody to Hell. If I send someone a letter, there is no action taken by the letter. The letter had no choice but to be sent. But God gave us free will to choose what we do, how we act, and what we believe (or don't believe) just to name a few. So people aren't sent to Hell. They end up there by their own choice.

The Bible tells us that we have all sinned and fallen short of God's standard (Rom. 3:23). The penalty of our sin is being eternally separated from Him, which is Hell. But God loved us enough to send Jesus to die in our place, and by accepting what He did for us on the cross, we can be forgiven as if we never sinned.

Well, what about people who don't believe in God or don't believe there is enough evidence for God? The Bible addresses that too, whether people agree with it or not. Romans 1:18–20 (TPT) says, "For God in heaven unveils his holy anger breaking forth against every form of sin, both toward ungodliness that lives in hearts and evil actions. *For the wickedness of humanity deliberately smothers the truth and keeps people*

> *from acknowledging the truth about God.* In reality, the truth of God is known instinctively, for God has embedded this knowledge inside every human heart. *Opposition to truth cannot be excused on the basis of ignorance,* because from the creation of the world, the invisible qualities of God's nature have been made visible, such as his eternal power and transcendence. *He has made his wonderful attributes easily perceived, for seeing the visible makes us understand the invisible. So then, this leaves everyone without excuse"* (my emphasis in italics added).
>
> I vividly remember the moment in my heart when I knew there was a God. I was only seven or eight years old. Yes, I'd been to church and Sunday school my entire life, but it didn't happen there. My family and I were on vacation in the mountains, and we were driving on the parkway. I was sitting behind my dad in the backseat of my parent's beige station wagon with wood paneling down the side (ah, the beautiful automobiles of the late 70s and early 80s). There was no discussion about God or church taking place, but I remember us rounding a corner when the most breathtaking view of a valley surrounded by tree-covered mountains appeared. I was in awe. At that very moment, even as a young child, I knew beyond a shadow of a doubt there was a God. To me, He was clearly seen. In the majesty of His creation, He was visible.
>
> I believe we have all experienced Him in a way to believe that He exists. Whether we choose to follow that truth is up to us. In his book, The Great Divorce, C.S. Lewis sums it up perfectly: "There are only two kinds of people in the end: those who say to God, 'Thy will be done,' and those to whom God says, in the end, 'Thy will be done.' All that are in Hell, choose it."

At first I was confused. I was thinking *That has to be a mistake, God. Are You sure?* I mean, I went to church three years in a row without missing a single Sunday. How could I be going to Hell? But going to McDonald's doesn't make you a Big Mac, and going to church doesn't make you a Christian, a believer, or Heaven-bound. It just makes you a churchgoer.

In my high school, most of my friends and teachers knew me as the good Christian kid. In fact, my senior year of high school, I took a class called Independent Living. Mrs. Debbie Grubbs was our teacher and was as sweet as they came. One assignment we did was take a list of 18 things and rank them from 1 to 18 in order of importance as guiding principles of our lives. Examples of things on the list were an exciting life, family security, a sense of accomplishment, self respect, and wisdom. Out of every student in all of her classes that school year, only one chose salvation/eternal life as the number one guiding principle of their lives—me. I remember being surprised that nobody else had chosen it as number one. But just saying eternal life was my top priority didn't cut it. Being a good person didn't cut it. Shoot, even believing in God didn't cut it.

There's one way to Heaven, and that's Jesus. He told us so in John 14:6, "...I am the way, the truth, and the life. No one comes to the Father except through Me." I've shared John 10:10 many times in this book, but in the verse prior, Jesus says, "I am the door. If anyone enters by Me, he will be saved..." (John 10:9).

After the shock of what God had just spoken to me sank in, I got really scared. If it wasn't for God's grace and goodness, that same goodness I'd heard the missionary to Africa preach about years earlier, I'd be burning in Hell. The good churchgoing kid whose number one priority in life was eternal life was busting the gates of Hell wide open.

And then a second, very deep, very dark fear struck me. How many people are on their way to Hell like I was and they have no idea??? How many are faithful to sit on a church pew every Sunday and maybe even toss a $20 in the collection plate as it passes, but have never asked Jesus to be their Lord and Savior? How many people are members of their church and believe that secures their eternal salvation? How many won't get a second chance like I did?

Those verses God led me to in Summer's pink Bible from Job 32 had just come to pass. I was set to take the stage in less than 10 minutes and I knew exactly what I was supposed to share. The tears were drying up. I was still in shock, but resolute to deliver what God had just spoken to me.

When I finally took the stage and parked myself behind the mic, it was obvious I'd been crying as I was still fighting back tears, but I didn't care. There were people in that gym going to Hell, and I wanted to do something about it. I addressed my tears quickly.

"I don't cry. You can ask my friends who are here tonight and they'll tell you. But I started crying when the candles were lit even though I didn't know any of these people," as I gestured toward the candles. "There's no reason for me to be crying."

I proceeded to share a very condensed version of how I lost my arm and found Jesus in the process, but added the new revelation God shared with me only moments earlier.

"God told me, 'If you would have died that day...'" And the tears resumed. I paused and looked at the floor of the stage through tear-stained eyes. I stood there for what seemed like minutes but was surely only seconds in reality. My voice quivered as I began again. "God told me, 'If you would have died that day, you would have gone to Hell.'"

The gym fell dead silent, except for a few sniffles from those in attendance who were brought to tears, including both Summer and Angela. My tears rushed back as I pleaded for no one to leave the gym that night without giving their lives to Jesus.

I found my seat as Clayton began his message. I honestly don't remember a whole lot of what he said. I was still in shock and thankful for my second chance. I do remember Clayton giving an altar call at the end of service and more than 70 people asked Jesus to be their personal Lord and Savior.

A burning passion for the lost was birthed in me that night in the gym of Alexander Central High School in Taylorsville, North Carolina. In that town of 2,241 people, I made a statement to God that has taken me across the United States and around the world sharing my testimony and preaching.

"God, I will do this every day for the rest of my life if it will keep just one person from going to Hell."

More than 23 years later as of the writing of this book, I'm still preaching and countless thousands have come to know Jesus as Lord. I've led complete strangers to Jesus. I've lead people to

Jesus on phone calls and through emails. I've led family members to Jesus. I led a close friend to Jesus a few years before she passed away from cancer. There's no greater experience than leading others to Jesus, and I have no intention of ever stopping.

CHAPTER 13

A NEW LOVE INTEREST

In the spring of 1998, I graduated from Appalachian State University with a Bachelor of Science in Applied Communication with a triple concentration in Organizational Communication, Public Communication, and Interpersonal Communication. After reading that you probably picture me snapping my suspenders and sliding my nerd glasses up the bridge of my nose, right? I'm not going to lie, that sounds pretty impressive and looks great on a resumé, but I had to sort through some old papers to even remember what my concentrations were. The only class I really benefited from was Public Speaking.

After graduation, I loaded all of my personal effects into my Blazer and started the drive down Highway 421 en route to my hometown. With my courses at college finished and some legal proceedings related to my accident delaying my job hunt, I started working on another course—the golf course. After my accident, one of the things I missed the most, other than my right arm, was competition. I'd played baseball since I was old enough to wear cleats and a glove, but that was no longer an option. My dad was an avid golfer, and I'd play a few times a year with him as I grew up. About one month after my accident, I went to The Lodge Golf Course in Laurinburg with him and three of his buddies. Like I wrote back in chapter 4, when you're from a small town, news spreads fast. But so does benevolence. My dad and his friends were playing in a tournament to benefit me. There are a few things that still stand out to me about that day.

The first was the sheer number of people who showed up to play. The course was packed with friends, my dad's coworkers, and complete strangers. People just wanted to help out and show support any way that they could. The second memory was how many people picked on me for bringing a pillow to the golf course. "Do you plan on taking a nap?" and "Do you find golf that boring?" were a couple of jabs I took that day. I know a pillow is a weird accessory to take to the links, but I'd been out of the hospital for just a few weeks and had to keep my arm elevated so I carried a king-size pillow with me practically everywhere I went to prop up my arm. My third memory took place on the green of the 12th hole. One of the guys in my dad's foursome was lining up a 15-foot putt when he looked up at me as I held the flagstick.

He extended his putter toward me and said, "Jeff, I don't feel like putting on this hole. Will you putt for me?" I'd never attempted a putt with only one hand, but I accepted the challenge. My dad held the flagstick as I gripped the putter. Everyone's eyes were fixated and hopes high as I rolled the ball toward the hole. I think all five of us were pulling for at least a small victory in my life at the moment. As the ball slid just right of the cup, my dad watched me. It was the first time he saw the competitive fire in my eyes since my last game on the diamond.

On the drive home from the course, he asked if I wanted to learn how to play golf again. After the initial question of, "Do you think I can?" I decided to give it a shot. As a reminder, I was right handed prior to my accident. I wasn't very coordinated or strong with my left arm, so learning how to swing the club would be difficult. The first few months my dad and I hit the range, I spent practically all of my time chipping and putting. I developed a strong short game while also building strength in my left arm. After five or six months, I started attempting full shots. I had my fair share of naysayers come out of the woodwork during this time, some telling my father it was cruel to even introduce me to the game. One guy told me, "Golf is a hard enough game with two arms. I can't even imagine trying to play with one. Maybe you should stop trying now before it gets too frustrating." While some might use that as an excuse to quit, I used it as motivation. Any time I felt extremely frustrated, I remembered those words and kept swinging.

Within 10 months, if I hit my driver as hard and straight as I could, the ball would max out around 150 yards. Around that time my dad birthed a pretty cool idea. My first round of golf would be on the one-year anniversary of my accident. We would tee off at 1:40 p.m., the approximate time the auger's teeth grabbed the glove on my right hand.

I was a nervous wreck as I stepped to the first tee on July 22, 1994. At 1:40 p.m., Mike Greenway, the club pro, announced me on the first tee like I was teeing it up at The Masters on the PGA Tour. Before I took my first swing, I'd set a goal of shooting no worse than 120; mind you, my lowest round with two arms was 90.

My first round with one arm could be best described as a guy chasing a white rock through a field while hitting it with a stick. It was ugly! But somehow I found myself standing on the 18th green staring at a five-footer. If I made it, I'd shoot 120 on the number; if I missed, 121. The nerves I experienced on the first tee rushed back. You would have thought the putt was for $1 million. My hand shook as I pulled the putter away and sent the ball toward the cup. It began to veer offline, and my heart sank; I wasn't going to meet my goal. But the ball held its line, barely caught the right lip and curled in the back of the hole. I'd done it! Although it felt like a terrible round, I'd accomplished my goal and sank a clutch putt to do so. It was nice to experience a victory, even if it was a small and ugly one.

And with that, my love for golf was born. I practiced regularly. Within six months, I broke 100 for the first time. A few years later I proved to be a better golfer with one arm than I was with two as I shot the first round of my life in the 80s. Within a couple more years, I started regularly shooting in the 70s. I even started competing in amputee golf tournaments across the country, winning the arm division in North Carolina and California in back-to-back tournaments. One thing I noticed in all of the amputee tournaments I played, whether I won or not, was I seemed to hit the ball quite a bit farther than most of my competitors.

Honestly, I had no idea the places this game would take me.

CHAPTER 14

MY WRITING CAREER BEGINS

In the beginning of 2001, the legal issues surrounding my accident finally reached a conclusion and I was able to commence my hunt for a career. I still didn't know what I wanted to be when I grew up, so I applied for a lot of different jobs. Some said yes, and I said no. Others said no when I really wanted a yes.

I had two job interviews lined up within a five-day period in my hometown. One was at *The Laurinburg Exchange*, the local newspaper I had appeared in many times throughout my life, mostly for what I did on the diamond as a kid growing up. A couple of articles about my accident and my life afterwards ended up in the paper as well. I didn't know much about being a reporter, but knew I had the ability to write so it seemed like a viable option.

The other interview I'd arranged was with the American Red Cross. When I lost my arm, the amount of blood I lost was astounding, so if it wasn't for organizations like the Red Cross and their blood drives, I might not have survived. I was thankful for the organization and wanted to help them if they'd have me.

Honestly, I'd have been happy if either offered me a position.

My interview with the newspaper was on a Thursday. I didn't have a writing portfolio to hand the editor, so a few days earlier, I attended a local high school baseball game and wrote an article as if I was a reporter. I turned the article in the day before my interview so the editor could have an idea of what kind of reporter I could be.

When I sat down in his office the next day, I felt extremely confident. I knew I could write, and I showed initiative by writing an article of my own. About 10 minutes into the interview, however, all of my confidence could have been put into a paper shredder like rough drafts of an article. I didn't feel like it was going well at all. The most damaging questions were about what writing experience I had and any writing classes I had taken in college. I was nearly to the point of apologizing for wasting his time on reading my resumé and interviewing me when his office door opened, I felt a slap on my back, and heard someone say, "Bardelli, how are you?"

"I'm good, Mike. How are you?"

It was the newspaper's publisher, Mike Milligan. His son, Benji, and I played baseball growing up together, played high school baseball together, and graduated high school together. He walked around the desk and stood next to the editor. The room fell silent as he glanced over my resumé. The next words out of his mouth changed the entire tone of the interview.

"I'm going to take a chance on you," he said. "Can you start Monday?"

"I sure can," I answered with a smile.

I left that interview and stopped by the Red Cross on my way home. I wanted to cancel my interview in person. The director was disappointed, but told me she understood. Before I left, she did mention that my interview was a mere formality because she knew she was going to hire me already.

This is one of those instances where I believe, as a believer, God nudged me in a certain direction, knowing this would shape my life and open up opportunities for me in the future. If I was hired by the Red Cross, I'm not confident this book would be in your hands right now because it more than likely would never have been written. I can't tell you how many times throughout the writing process I've relied on wisdom I learned in my 15+ year writing career.

So, with *zero* writing experience, I learned to be a newspaper reporter as a newspaper reporter. And the crazy thing is my career nearly ended before it even began as I was given the most difficult of assignments my third day on the job. A young teacher, who was a mother of two, had been murdered and I was asked to interview the family. That was hard enough, but I was also told to ask a few questions that would be considered less than flattering about the victim. I just knew I couldn't ask those questions to grieving family members. I sat at my desk and stared at my office phone. One call to the American Red Cross and I could start a new career within a couple of days.

Mike walked behind me as I sat at my desk. "My office. Now."

Apparently he heard I was ready to call it quits. By the time I reached his office, he was already seated behind his desk covered in papers.

"Close the door and have a seat," he said rather sternly.

Great, I thought. *He's going to fire me before I even have a chance to quit.*

"I hear you're thinking about quitting."

"Yes sir," I replied.

"Why?"

"I was told to interview the family of the teacher who was just murdered and ask some questions that don't seem kind or fair," I answered. "That doesn't seem right."

"I told the editor to assign that interview to you," he replied. "Do you want to know why?"

I was thinking *You believe you made a mistake hiring me* or *You don't like me and want me gone*. I answered, "Yes sir."

He said, "I told him to give you that assignment because I knew you would go in there as a Christian first and as a reporter second. As far as the unfair questions, don't ask those. Just write a good story about her. Can you do that?"

"Yes sir, I can. And thank you."

I interviewed the family and wrote the article, one of the better articles I wrote as a reporter. (Side note: eventually the killer was caught and sentenced to life in prison.) I'm very thankful for that conversation in my boss' office. From that talk, I worked as a reporter for nearly a year and a half, honed my skills as a writer, got my foot in the door for my next job, and eventually started writing the book you're holding right now.

CHAPTER 15

MY NEXT CHAPTER

It seemed like any other day in the office for me in May 2002. I'd been a reporter for more than a year and had really found my niche. I'd settled in as the crime reporter and got to cover an occasional sporting event. Perched behind my desk in my small cubicle one morning, my fingers were clicking away at the keyboard, putting the finishing touches on an article for the following day's paper. Working for the newspaper was a lot like having a second-shift job. I typically came to work between noon and two p.m. and left anywhere between 8 p.m. and midnight. This particular day, however, was different as I was already working on an article by 11 a.m. I was reading through my notes when, out of absolutely nowhere, God spoke to me. It wasn't audible like I'd heard before, but there was no mistaking it was Him. I wasn't sitting at my desk praying or even thinking about God or anything spiritual. I was working. But I unmistakably heard, "Go to Rhema." Again, I didn't hear it audibly, but I "heard" it on the inside.

For those unfamiliar, Rhema (pronounced ray-muh) is Rhema Bible Training College, located in Broken Arrow, Oklahoma, just on the outskirts of Tulsa in the northeast part of the state. A few years earlier, I considered attending Bible college. I even applied and was accepted to one in Ohio, but, in the end, didn't feel like that's where I was supposed to go. I'd since put Bible college on the back-burner and hadn't thought much about it. So it came as a shock to me when I heard "Go to Rhema" out of nowhere.

I initially thought *You go to Rhema. I'm fine where I'm at.* But I heard it again, "Go to Rhema." This time, I immediately picked up my desk phone and called my pastor, Daryl Cook, to see if he could join me for lunch that day.

"When?" he said.

"Is an hour too soon?" I replied.

Within an hour, we were sitting across the table from each

other at a restaurant in downtown Laurinburg. It even shared a parking lot with *The Laurinburg Exchange.*

"What did you want to talk to me about?" Daryl asked. He was 30 years old when he became the pastor of my church, although he looked like he was 18 (and that number might be a little generous). He was a 1991 Rhema graduate, so I knew I could go to him with any questions. But first, I had to share the news with him.

"I'm going to Rhema. God told me to go this morning."

He just smiled. "I knew you were going to say that. I knew as soon as you asked me if we could eat lunch." We spent the remainder of lunch talking about his experience at RBTC and what my next steps were. Within a couple of weeks, my application and references were in the mail. Now it was just a waiting game to see when I'd be accepted. I knew God told me to go, so there was no doubt I'd get in.

Not one to let grass grow under my feet, I started planning a trip to Oklahoma with my pastor so he could show me around and help me find a place to live. We decided to make the 17-hour drive overnight to avoid heavy traffic through the larger cities along I-40 and to maximize our time in Broken Arrow. I was saying goodbye to my mom and stepdad standing in the front yard of their house when the mailman delivered our mail that day. My acceptance letter came mere minutes before we departed, which really came in handy because it granted me access to things on campus that otherwise would have been closed off.

Sending in that application and moving 17 hours away from home to a town where I knew no one was the beginning of a faith walk that I've been walking ever since. In fact, the last Sunday I was home before I left for Rhema, Pastor Daryl asked me to preach. The title of my message?

A Faith Walk Begins With Just One Step.

Moving 17 hours away was difficult. Leaving all of my family and friends behind was very difficult. But sitting through three hours of Bible classes every day was amazing! To be honest, when I left for Rhema, I felt like I already knew a lot about the Bible. I never missed a church service and, not only did I read, but I studied my Bible daily. Within the first two days—maybe within the first two minutes of my first class—I realized how much I didn't know. But like one of my instructors said, "It's what you learn after you already know it all that really makes the difference."

Not only was I learning, growing, and making new friends, but I found out Rhema had an intercollegiate golf team and tryouts were coming soon. You mean, I can attend Bible college, grow in my knowledge of God, *and* not only play competitive golf, but play it for free? #SignMeUp

Enter Tad Gregurich. He was an instructor at Rhema, but also the school's golf coach. I'm not sure what he thought when he saw a one-armed guy show up to try out for the golf team, but after I hit my second shot out of a fairway bunker on the first hole from 155 yards with a 7-iron over water and onto the green, he was convinced I could play. I wish I could spend the remainder of this chapter talking about my amazing exploits on the golf course the following two seasons, about all of the tournaments I won, and how sponsors were knocking my door down hoping to sign me to a contract before I joined the PGA Tour, but I was pedestrian at best. If I could have kept my nerves in check, I'd have been a much better golfer. However, I was the best one-armed golfer in every tournament we played in, so there's that.

The highlights of my two-year golf career at Rhema were finishing second in a tournament in Arkansas and co-holding the school record for most eagles in a career with two. My first came after holing my second shot on a par 4 from 113 yards. My second was on a par 5 where I hit my second shot onto the green from 244 yards out with a 4-wood and followed it up by draining a 20-foot putt that broke 6 feet from right to left. The funny thing about that eagle was I was so excited to see that putt drop that I tried to do a fist pump. My left hand was occupied with my putter, so I gave a fist pump with my non-existent right hand. In other words, I basically just moved what was left of my right arm up and down aggressively about three times.

Every tournament we went to, when I started warming up on the driving range, the majority of other competitors stopped for a little while and watched me. Multiple guys came up to me during my two years playing and said something to the effect of, "I think it's really impressive what you're doing. I know I couldn't do that (and I watched as many tried and failed). But I don't care if everybody else beats me as long as I don't get beat by you." With that thought echoing in my head, I heaped pressure on my own shoulders by thinking I had to play well every single round just to prove myself, but that didn't work at all. If everyone had to compete with only one arm, I would have dominated, but, unfortunately for me, we never played by those rules.

I was always the most nervous on the first tee. Most golfers are, but so many people stopped what they were doing when my name was announced to see what the one-armed guy would do. Our first tournament in Kansas stands out in particular. The putting green was within just a few yards of the first tee and it was loaded with golfers ready to start their rounds. After the group in front of us were walking toward the resting place of their initial shots, I grabbed my bag and stepped to the tee box. I immediately pulled out my driver, started spinning the shaft of the club in my hand so quickly I nearly became airborne, and began pacing. I continued this for many minutes, waiting on the group in front of us to clear so we could tee it up.

I'm not sure if I'd ever been more nervous in my life, except for maybe the first time I shared my testimony. It didn't help matters at all that I'd just watched a teammate in the previous group hit his opening tee shot out of bounds, rolling his Titleist into someone's rose bushes directly in front of their house. Tad, who I always refer to as "Coach" even though he's a pastor, doctor, and the current dean of Rhema, knew my nerves got the best of me, so he always tried his best to settle me down. A couple of minutes before I teed off, he joined me on the tee box with a serious look on his face. He was a great golfer in his own right, so I expected to get a pep talk, a pointer about the hole, or advice on where to hit my tee shot.

I was way off.

He leaned in and whispered, "You realize you only have one arm, right?"

I belly laughed! It was the perfect comment at the perfect moment, and it calmed me down. When it was my turn to pull the trigger, I piped my tee shot down the middle of the fairway about 270 yards. I looked at Coach and grinned, "Not bad for one arm, huh?"

All he could do was laugh. As I scooped my bag up and started down the fairway, the starter joined me for a few steps. He told me about a couple of tricky holes on the course before shaking my hand and telling me I was his new hero.

Stories and experiences like that with Coach are why he is one of my closest friends to this day. In fact, he and his wife, Amanda, along with their two kids, Emily and Tanner, kind of adopted me into their family during my 10-year stint in Oklahoma. If I was in town, I was invited to every holiday celebration except for Groundhog Day, which I celebrate privately (hopefully fans of my favorite television show, *The Office*, caught that reference). When Tanner turned nine and had a birthday party, he invited eight other nine year olds and me. Yep, I was playing baseball in the backyard with eight nine year olds. Yep, I ate cake and ice cream with eight nine year olds. Yep, I jumped on the trampoline with eight nine year olds. I just happened to be 29 at the time and had a lot less energy (and arms) than they did.

This little family was about to change my life with a seemingly innocent Christmas present, and the present wasn't even for me.

CHAPTER 16

SOMETIMES RECORDS BREAK

It was Christmas 2004. Tad and Amanda decided to give their son, Tanner, a gift they knew he'd love. As a fourth grader, Tanner was slightly obsessed with the *Guinness Book of World Records*. Any time his class was in the library, he'd make a beeline for a copy and start reading through all of the different records, but especially the sports section. Honestly, I remember doing the same thing when I was his age, but the only record I still remember was the world's heaviest twins and a picture of them riding motorcycles together (FYI, it was Billy and Benny McCrary, they weighed in at 723 and 745 pounds, and a quick Google search will reveal the motorcycle picture). Tanner's mom, Amanda, heard him constantly talking about the book every day after school, so he was surprised with the newest edition on Christmas morning.

One day, Tanner was flipping through the pages of the sports section and he froze. Moments later, he was running through his house yelling for his dad. When he found him, he laid the book open in front of him and pointed. It was the record for the longest carry of a golf ball with one hand. The record was 236.22 yards by Petri Takkunen of Finland. He set the standard on June 16, 2003. When Tad saw that number, he grabbed his cell phone and punched in my number.

He told me what Tanner had found. "You can beat that. I've seen you hit it farther than that in tournaments."

"I don't know, Coach," I replied. "That's a long way."

He was unflinching. "I've seen you do it!"

"Yeah, but that was with the bounce and roll. I don't think I can hit it that far in the air."

Unfazed, he answered, "You can do it. I know you can. I've watched you do it!"

When someone believes in you that much, you've got to try at least. So I answered, "I guess it's time to start practicing." Within an hour, I was at the driving range banging drives as far as I could.

I spent the next few months practicing three to five days a week. I was trying everything—different clubs and stances, teeing the ball at different heights, various swing thoughts—in an attempt to gain an extra yard or two. As I practiced, I could never tell exactly how far the ball was traveling in the air. I had a good idea of my total distance once the ball stopped rolling, but trying to pinpoint an exact yardage where the ball first hit the ground from over two football fields away is practically impossible. You might be thinking *Why didn't you have someone stand on the driving range to see where the ball landed and measure it from there?* Well, every time I went to the range, there were multiple people practicing. I couldn't send a buddy out there to spot the ball's landing point and risk them getting beaned by someone else.

Half the time I went to the range, someone would join me to watch my swing and offer any pointers on how I could hit it further. Remember, the record was for how far the ball flew in the air, not just how far I could hit it. The bounce and roll wouldn't count. If it did, I would have gone to the airport and hit the ball down a runway. I wasn't swinging my typical swing. I was swinging a lot harder and trying to hit the ball higher. I benefited a lot from tapping into the wisdom of others, but my best day of practice happened when I was all by myself.

It was just like any other day at the range. I had finished my warm up of hitting a few wedges to loosen up my back. I pulled my driver out and started launching balls down the range. I have a habit of standing behind the ball before every shot to pick out a target. I'd developed the habit years earlier and it was something I passed on to all of the golf teams I coached after I graduated from player to assistant coach to head coach. I would ask my guys, "If you're not aiming at anything specific, how do you know if you actually hit a good shot? Yes, you might hit it 300 yards, but did it go in the direction you were aiming?"

As I stood on the range that day, I was lining up a shot when God spoke to me.

#TEACHABLEMOMENT
When God "Speaks"

I feel like a #TeachableMoment is absolutely necessary here. I don't want you to think God speaks to me all the time. Far from it. It's actually pretty rare for me. I do feel like I get a nudge or leading from Him regularly, but I wouldn't say he regularly "speaks" to me. I've heard Him audibly once, but mostly when he speaks, I "hear" it on the inside.

For the purposes of this book, I've shared most of them because they are such a major component of my story. I do believe God speaks to people, but if I am around people who claim God is constantly "talking" to them, I get a little wary. Some people claim God talks to them frequently and I believe it could be for a few reasons. (For this discussion, I'm not talking about the ministry gift of a prophet as you read in Ephesians 4:11.)

1. They want to appear spiritually superior to everyone around them. Many times these people are so heavenly minded they are no earthly good. I'm not saying they never hear from God. I'm just saying I don't think they hear from Him **that** much. The dangers with people like this are some people will actually believe everything they say and take it as if God Himself is saying it. I've heard stories of people saying, "God told me you are going to marry this person and you'll have six children" (or some very similar version). And then when that doesn't happen, they figure they missed God and don't know what to do with their lives.

Others might doubt their own ability to hear from God because they don't hear from Him as much as Brother So-and-so or Sister Such-and-such. There was a person who was a part of the college ministry I attended right after I got saved who always "heard from God." Seemingly every Monday night when we had our services, she would approach our campus pastor and tell him God had given her a message for the group. Occasionally, he would let her share what she received. In a candid moment I had with the campus pastor, I shared my frustration about my inability to hear from God in comparison to this person. He said that many times, he didn't believe she'd actually heard from God and that's when he wouldn't give her the mic, but occasionally he believed she did and would let her share. It seemed like she wanted everyone to think she was more spiritual than them. She had a "spiritual superiority complex."

2. They want to excuse their actions or desires by saying, "that's what God told me to do or not to do." You might hear statements like, "God told me to buy this car," or "God told me to quit my job." Now, I'm not saying that either of those statements has never been uttered by Him, but I guarantee you they haven't been said nearly as much as people claimed to have heard it. In fact, when I was in college, a girl approached me and said, "God told me you were going to be my husband." Well, that was news to me. I responded with, "If He told you, He will have to tell me too." He didn't. Did I miss God? Nope! Had she actually heard from God? Again, nope! She just saw this one-armed goodness and wanted it all for herself! So when someone "hears" from God, I usually measure it against what kind of motivation or ulterior motive there might be behind it.

With that in mind, if you believe you have heard from God, judge it by a few standards. First, and most importantly, does it line up with what the Bible says? If it doesn't, you didn't hear from Him. Period. Exclamation point! HARD STOP. End of story. God will never tell you anything that contradicts His Word. Ever. Second, if it does line up with the Bible, do you have any underlying motive for why you hope God told you something? Yes, the Bible tells us in Genesis 2:18 that it's not good for man to be alone, so if you desire to be married,

> God desires that too. But He would never tell you that your spouse is someone who is already married, no matter how good looking they are or how perfect they might seem for you. That's just weird. And stupid. Don't be weird and stupid.

So, as I was lining up a shot on the driving range that day, God spoke to me. Again, I wasn't praying or doing anything spiritual. I was hitting golf balls. When all of a sudden I heard on the inside, "You sure are working hard to get your name in that book." It caught me by surprise and made me think. I had been working hard to break the record to hopefully get my name in the *Guinness Book of World Records*. I'd been at the range multiple days a week, hitting hundreds of balls each day trying to get better. I knew there had to be a point behind God saying that to me, so I answered, "Yes, I am. What about it?"

He replied, "But there's one book you didn't have to work at all to get your name into — the Lamb's Book of Life. Jesus did all the work for you. You just have to accept what He did for you on the cross."

I started smiling. I still wanted to break the world record, but if I didn't get my name in the *Guinness Book of World Records*, my name was forever written in the most important book — the Lamb's Book of Life (Rev. 13:8; 21:27). By not rejecting Jesus, my name is forever written in the roster of Heaven, and my eternal life is guaranteed.

Now, if you've skipped the other #TeachableMoments, I'm going to ask you to please read this one. I promise it's worth it!

#TEACHABLEMOMENT
Is Your Name in That Book?

This is *by far* the most important #TeachableMoment of the entire book. It's a simple question that requires a simple answer. If you can't give a simple answer, your answer is more than likely "No." Have you accepted what Jesus did for you on the cross and asked Him to be your personal Lord and Savior?

Maybe you're reading this and you don't know exactly what He did for you. John 3:16 says, "For God so loved the world, that he gave his only Son, that whoever believes in him should not perish but have eternal life" (ESV). And my favorite verse in the entire Bible is Romans 5:8, which says, "But God demonstrates His own love toward us, in that while we were still sinners, Christ died for us." One day I was studying this verse when I saw it in a completely different light. To be more accurate, I saw it from two different perspectives.

Notice the first part of the verse: "But God demonstrates His own love toward us, in that while we were still sinners..." If you can think of the worst sin you believe you've ever committed, God loved you enough while you were in the very act of sinning to send His Son to die on the cross for you and your sins. That is absolutely amazing love! Now, look at the second half of that verse: "...while we were still sinners, Christ died for us." Again, if you can think of the worst sin you believe you've ever committed, Jesus loved you enough while you were in the very act of sinning to give His life for you on the cross. That is just an amazingly ridiculous love. And He did that knowing full well some would reject His act of love and even mock Him. I mean, that started while He was still hanging on the cross (see Matt. 27:39–44) and He forgave them in that very moment (see Luke 23:34).

My friend, Jesus loves you! Yes, you! And God isn't mad at you for anything you have done in your past. You might be saying, "But Jeff, you don't know what I've done." You're right. I don't know what you've done, but I do know what Jesus did and how much God loves you. I know Jesus died on the cross for your sins to bring you close to God. First Peter 3:18 says, "Christ suffered for our sins once for all time.

> He never sinned, but he died for sinners to bring you safely home to God" (NLT).
>
> If you can't think back to a specific time when you asked Jesus to be the Lord of your life, there's never a better time to do it than right now. Or maybe you do remember, but you've walked away from God and you know you're not living the way you're supposed to. You can rededicate your life to Him at this very moment. The Bible tells us in Romans 10:9–10, "If you openly declare that Jesus is Lord and believe in your heart that God raised him from the dead, you will be saved. For it is by believing in your heart that you are made right with God, and it is by openly declaring your faith that you are saved" (NLT).
>
> If you'd like to make Jesus your personal Lord and Savior, simply pray this prayer out loud right where you are:
>
> *Dear God,*
> *I admit that I am a sinner and know my sin separates me from You. I believe Jesus came to Earth, He died for my sins, He rose from the dead, He is alive again, and I confess Him as my Lord. The Bible says that if I confess with my mouth and believe in my heart, I will be saved. I thank You for saving me.*
> *In Jesus name I pray,*
> *Amen.*
>
> If you prayed that prayer, I would love to hear from you. Would you please email me at **salvation@jeffbardel.com** so I can hear the good news and celebrate with you?

After months of practice, I decided it was time to try to break the world record. I contacted Guinness World Records to find out the parameters for breaking the record. There were basically two rules: the land had to be flat (and surveyed for proof) and there had to be at least six spotters to ensure someone saw the exact spot where the ball first contacted the ground, because the bounce and roll didn't count. Once I learned the rules, the only thing left to do was find a location. The driving range I'd been practicing at in Oklahoma seemed flat enough, so I spoke with the owner about attempting to break the record at his facility. He agreed, and we set a date and time.

On March 19, 2005, I showed up at the range a little early and started warming up. It was unusually warm for Oklahoma in March, so the driving range was packed. I was already extremely nervous because I was trying to do something *no one in the world had ever done before*, and a packed house at the driving range just made it worse. As I was warming up, I noticed a small group of people start to form about 15 yards behind me. I tried to ignore them and focus on what I was doing, but the group just stood there. Eventually I turned to look at them to see what they were doing when I realized quite a few of my friends and coworkers had come to cheer me on. I stopped warming up, walked over, and thanked everyone for coming. I didn't think it was possible, but as I returned to finish my warm up, I realized I was even more nervous than before.

At least I can't get any more nervous than this I thought.

I thought wrong.

As I continued my warm up, I was interrupted by a news crew who had learned of my record-breaking attempt and showed up with a television camera and reporter. I did a brief interview with them prior to finishing my warm up.

Thankfully, one of my good friends, one of the best golfers I've ever played with, and just an amazingly nice guy, Jonathan Beaver, was there to help me that day. Even with all of those accolades, "Beave" is one of those golfers you actually don't like because he makes everything look so easy when you know how difficult it actually is. He was always good for a pointer when my swing felt off (which was often), but, more importantly, he was so laid back he had a calming effect on me, which I desperately needed that day. But when it was time for me to pull the trigger on my first attempt at breaking the record, he came in handy in a completely different way.

The owner of the driving range made an announcement to let everyone know that a world record attempt was about to take place, so they needed to stop hitting balls for a few minutes to allow the spotters to get in place on a grid which had been painted on the range. So now, not only did I have a group of friends there to watch me, but the driving range was completely shut down while I swung. *No pressure, right?*

I took a couple of practice swings to settle my nerves, but faced a problem I hadn't foreseen. My hand was shaking so bad, I couldn't sit the ball on the tee. Thankfully, Beave told me to toss him the ball. For each of my six followings swings, he took care of the daunting task of teeing the ball up for me.

I stood behind the ball and picked out my target, basically aiming between the two spotters standing in the middle of the grid. I addressed the golf ball, took one last look at my target, quoted Philippians 4:13, and swung as hard as I could. I didn't make great contact, catching the ball toward the toe of the club. The ball started toward my target before it softly started drifting to the right. One of the spotters pointed at the ball as it started its descent toward the dry Oklahoma turf.

The ball struck the ground.

We watched, waited, and listened.

After what seemed like 10 minutes but was surely just a few seconds, the walkie-talkie in the owner's hand squelched and the distance was announced:

"248 yards."

I had just broken the world record by 12 yards on a shot I didn't hit very well. You would think everyone would be cheering like crazy, congratulating me, and patting me on the back, but because of the 15-yard gap between us and my group of friends, no one heard the distance announced except me, Beave, and the news crew.

The news crew didn't react. I didn't react. Beave just looked at me, grinned, and gave me a high-five. The group behind us just stood there staring. I turned around and meekly said, "I did it." I'm not sure why I didn't yell it or run to them and high-five everybody. Maybe it was shock. I'd practiced for months, hitting thousands of golf balls with different clubs, different stances, different tee heights, and with one swing, and not a particularly good one, I'd broken the record. I was stunned.

"What do I do now?" I said to no one in particular.

The reporter said, "Try to hit it farther." Sounded like a good idea.

Beave teed the next ball up, and I violently lashed at it, missing the grid waaaaaaaay left. I mean, it was left of left's third cousin twice removed. The next two swings weren't much better, but the fifth ball I hit a little better and waited for the announcement.

"251 yards."

I was done. I'd hit the ball more than two and a half football fields in the air, breaking the old record by 15 yards. I had done something no one in the world had ever done before.

Because a television crew was there that day, news spread pretty quickly. Within a day or two, I heard from people across the country who saw my record-breaking swing on various news outlets. Local stations carried it, as well as major news outlets like CNN and ESPN. Unfortunately, I didn't see any of them, and a few of my friends said ESPN got my name wrong, calling me Jeff Barnhill.

There was one step left to make the record official: get the land surveyed. I knew the land was flat enough. I teed off in front of the tee box so I was hitting from the same level as where the ball would land instead of from the elevated tee box. I was assured a surveyor was coming to the driving range within a couple days to confirm the distance and survey the land.

I was excited to get my information turned in to Guinness World Records, so after four or five days, I went to the driving range to see if the survey was completed. I could still see the small flag they'd stuck in the ground where my ball had landed. The owner explained the land hadn't been surveyed yet, but it would be soon. A few days later, I called and heard the same answer. I decided to give him a little more time before checking in again, so a week later I returned to the range hoping to leave with the survey in hand. As I walked up, I noticed the flag marking my drive was removed. *That's a good sign* I thought.

Again, I thought wrong.

I didn't get to speak with the owner that day, but instead with a member of his staff. I basically left with the impression that the land wouldn't be surveyed, and the exact location of where my ball struck the ground was no longer marked, so even if it was surveyed, it wouldn't do any good.

Talk about disappointment. I'd worked so hard to break the record, had actually done it, but it wouldn't be official because someone else dropped the ball. After stewing over it for a few weeks, I determined in my mind to break the record again. In fact, I not only decided to break the record again, but to hit it even farther than I did the first time. This time, however, I'd do it where I knew things would be done right from start to finish.

CHAPTER 17

SOMETIMES RECORDS BREAK: THE SEQUEL

It all started with a phone call.

Sitting at the desk in my office in Broken Arrow, Oklahoma, I grabbed my cell phone and called a golf course just a few minutes from my parent's house in Laurinburg, North Carolina.

"Scotch Meadows Pro Shop, this is Mike."

The voice I heard on the other end of the line was just the man I was looking for. Mike Greenway was the assistant golf pro at Scotch Meadows Country Club, the only private club in my hometown. When I was in elementary school, my dad was a member, partly to play golf, but mostly because it came with a pool membership. I still have fond memories of going to the course with him, but my favorite part was when we got to the 18th hole. The final hole was a dogleg right, par 5 with a creek that crossed the fairway just short of the green. My dad kept a stash of old golf balls in his bag for this very hole. Not for himself, but for me. After hitting his approach shot into the green, he'd drive the cart up to the creek, pull a few of the older balls out of his bag, and let me try to hit shots over the water onto the green. I was probably seven or eight years old at the time, and at that age, I'm not sure if it was more fun to hit balls over the water or into the water. If you were judging only by my results, you'd surely have guessed hitting them into the water was what I enjoyed best.

Prior to joining the staff at Scotch Meadows, Mike was the head pro at The Lodge Golf Course, which is where he and I formed a close friendship. I mentioned him in chapter 13 when he announced my name on the first tee for my first round with one arm.

Mike was one of those positive influences on my golf game. He worked with me from time to time, but was always there to offer a quick word of encouragement after a bad round. We even played a few matches against each other as my game improved. Even though he'll swear he didn't, I think he tossed a couple of matches my way to boost my confidence a little bit. Not only that, but Mike had an interesting story himself. My dad and I gave him the nickname "Flash" after he answered the phone at the course one day during a thunderstorm when he was alone in the pro shop. Thirty minutes later he woke up on the floor with a rare title: lightning strike survivor.

Mike joined the staff at Scotch Meadows a few years earlier after stepping down from his previous job. He already knew about me breaking the record because word spreads around a small town quickly. After some brief small talk and updates on where our lives were, I got down to the real reason for my call.

"I want to come home and break the record again," I told him. "Can you help me make it happen at Scotch Meadows?"

"Absolutely," he replied.

And with that, my second attempt to get into the *Guinness Book of World Records* began. This time around, I was much more confident. I'd already broken the record once and did so rather easily, so I knew I could do it again. My real goal was to hit it farther than I did the first time I broke it. The official record still stood at 236 yards, but 252 was my target.

I won't bore you with the details on how we set everything up, but I flew to North Carolina in July 2006. On the morning of July 19, I pulled into the parking lot at Scotch Meadows and was sitting on the back bumper of the car putting my golf shoes on when Mike walked up. Perfect timing.

"Hey, Mike, can you tie my shoes for me?" (For the record, I can tie my own shoes. It just takes me forever and I can never get them as tight as I want them.)

"No. Do it yourself."

He might have been a positive influence on my game, but he would still rib me any chance he got. After Mike got me laced up, I made my way to the driving range, the morning dew still sticking to the grass in most places. The range was a revolving door of guys of all age ranges, each hitting a few balls before they rode off to the first tee to start their rounds.

After getting loose, I hopped in my cart and drove back to the pro shop to let everyone know I was ready. Mike and the Head Pro,

Chip Wells, ruled out the driving range for my attempt, because I'd be hitting from a slightly elevated tee box which meant landing the ball on the ground at the same level as me would be next to impossible. After thinking about each of the 18 holes on the course, they decided the flattest hole for me to attempt the record on would be the 8th, a straight away par 5 that plays 455 yards from the tips. The only issue was the men's tee was slightly elevated above the fairway, so they moved me to the senior tee box, which placed me 100 yards closer to the hole but offered a teeing ground level to the surface where my ball should land. Because of the way the course wound around itself, the 8th tee was really convenient because it was less than 30 yards from the parking lot.

Standing on the 8th tee, I paused and took in my surroundings. Standing about 15 yards behind the tee box were my mom, stepdad, sister, brother-in-law, and my one-year-old niece, along with two of my cousins who were always and will always be like little brothers, William and John Campbell. To their left about 30 yards away was a large group of spectators, one being the owner of a local radio station who, unbeknownst to me, happened to be broadcasting my record-breaking attempt live on the air. A reporter and television cameraman were perched on the edge of the tee box, filming every single move I made. In the direction of the green were Chip and nine volunteer spotters ready to locate the exact spot my drive first struck the ground. Mike was standing on the tee with me at all times, because he knew it's a lonely feeling on a tee box all by yourself.

I squatted into a catcher's position, bowed my head, and talked to God.

A moment of prayer

I thanked Him for the abilities He'd given me and asked that I would perform to the best of those abilities. My nerves were there in full force. (Shoot, I'm even nervous typing this and I know how the story ends.) I didn't have butterflies in my stomach. It was more like pterodactyls, and there were a lot of them! Amazingly, I was able to tee the ball up on my own even though my hand was noticeably shaking.

The first time I broke the record I did so on my first swing, and not a particularly good one. I thought I'd do it again.

I thought wrong. (First swing.)

Very wrong. (Second swing.)

Extremely wrong. (Third swing.)

Terribly wrong. (Fourth swing.)

Horrendously wrong. (Fifth swing.)

Things weren't going well at all. My first shot is what many golfers refer to as a "worm burner," a ball that is hit really hard but barely leaves the ground. It's definitely not a record-breaking swing. My following four shots all missed the golf course. And that's not hyperbole. I literally missed the golf course. Out of bounds skirted the entire right side of the hole. I came closer to breaking a window than a record because a row of houses ran parallel to the fairway. My second shot definitely struck a house, but thankfully I didn't hear glass shatter.

After each swing I noticed how the spotters took a few steps toward me. At the rate I was going, I'd be able to shake their hands while still standing on the tee box in about five more swings.

I had to regroup. I was mad and embarrassed. I'd flown to North Carolina to break the record. A radio and television station showed up to cover a world record, and I hadn't hit a ball close enough to anyone to be measured yet. Doubt was starting to creep in and anger was coming to the surface. Half of me wished I could just disappear. The other half knew if I could channel this anger, I'd demolish a ball.

I put my head down and just stared at my feet. Mike walked over, put his head on top of mine, and said, "Calm down. You've got this. You've got it inside you. God put it there. You're here for a reason."

I teed the next one up, stood behind the ball, took a deep breath, picked out a target, and addressed the ball. I recited Philippians 4:13 in my head, one more deep breath, and pulled the trigger.

It wasn't solid contact, but at least it was headed in the right direction and it was airborne. The guys on the left edge of the fairway saw it and started jogging forward, not the direction I wanted to see them moving. The ball struck the ground in the left rough a couple of feet to the right of a spotter. Chip jogged over, range finder in hand. He set the laser on me and we waited. The walkie talkie in Mike's hand squelched.

"238 yards."

I'd broken the record by two yards. Mike announced the record to my family and the group of onlookers. They all cheered, but I was mad.

238 yards??? I thought. 238 freaking yards??? Last time I hit it 251. Come on, Jeff! Hit the ball like you know you can!

The next three shots I hooked into the trees on the left because I was swinging mad and I was getting tired. I tried to settle down, but hit the next two shots thin. I hit them in the fairway, but not very long.

Mike tossed me a ball and said, "This is the last ball I've got. I can go get more."

I didn't answer. I was exhausted. I hadn't slept well the night before, I'd already hit a bucket of balls to warm up, and I'd put everything I had into my last 11 swings. I didn't know how much I had left, but 252 was still my goal. I knew it would only take one solid swing.

I teed up the Titleist Pro V1 and went through my routine.

Come on, Jeff. You've got this!

I took the club back, slow transition from my takeaway to my downswing, and the club struck the ball.

THWACK!

The record-breaking swing

The sound of impact echoed off the trees framing the tee box and fairway. From that sound alone, I knew I'd done it. I barely felt the club hit the ball. I'd hit the sweet spot. The ball launched into the air, and my cousin, William, started jumping up and down yelling, "Get off me ball! Get off me ball!" He knew I'd caught it too.

The ball started down the center of the fairway and slowly started turning ever so slightly to the left. Once the ball started its descent, I turned my attention to the spotters. They were running in the opposite direction. I smiled. I knew this was going to be a good number.

The ball landed in the left center of the fairway. Chip wasn't even in position to give us the yardage yet, but his voice echoed out of the walkie in Mike's hand.

"That was HUGE!" he yelled.

My family heard his announcement and started going crazy, jumping up and down and cheering louder than anyone had ever cheered on that course. Mike motioned for them to keep it down so he could hear the announcement of the yardage. I kept my eyes focused on Chip. I wanted to know the number. Chip got in position, focused his range finder on me, and made the announcement.

"Congratulations, 263 yards."

I gave Mike a high-five reminiscent of the one Tiger gave his caddie, Steve Williams, after holing out a chip on the 16th hole in the 2005 edition of The Masters. In other words, it was slightly awkward. Our hands were at weird angles, and we were both really excited. I didn't care. I'd done it. I knew the land would be surveyed, and I would be the official world record holder.

The land was surveyed within a few days, and the official yardage came back at 258 yards, 2 feet, 4 inches. Honestly, as long as it was 251 yards and 1 inch, I'd have been happy.

This all happened on a Wednesday. Thursday night, I was sitting in my parent's living room alone watching Sportscenter on ESPN. Toward the end of the episode, the Top Plays (top 10) came on, which has always been one of my favorite segments. The next thing I saw, to my surprise, was my face on the screen. I was number 5 in the top 10 plays. Apparently the news report about my swing had made its way to Bristol, Connecticut, the home of ESPN's headquarters. I couldn't believe it. I started yelling for my family to come see. By the time they reached the living room, I was no longer on the screen. They asked me what was said. I told them I had no clue because as soon as I saw my face I started screaming for them to come see.

The good (or bad) thing about Sportscenter is if you miss it in one episode, the same episode will be replayed, but they'll add any new updates since the previous episode aired. My family was glued to the screen with the VCR ready to record. When Top Plays came on, we hit record, but something happened within the hour that was better than what I had done and I had fallen to number 6.

I had made it on to ESPN again, and they got my name wrong—again. The first time I broke the record they called me Jeff Barnhill. This time, I was Steve Bardel. I earned the nickname Steve Barnhill for a while. Someone asked me if I was going to try to break the record again, and I told them with a laugh, "I'm going to keep breaking it until ESPN gets my name right."

I was getting all of the paperwork ready to submit to Guinness when a buddy of mine contacted me with some bad news. A two-armed golfer named Cristian Sterning, who competes in long drive competitions around the world, took one hand off the club and hit the ball a long way in the air—282 yards to be exact. That's almost a quarter of a football field longer than I had hit it.

I knew that was probably out of my range. I could hit one in the 270s (Mike thought my record-breaking drive would have been over 270 if the wind was at my back instead of in my face), but reaching 282 would be extremely difficult. (Even as I write this I can't type the word "impossible," because I don't allow that word into my vocabulary often.)

Would it have been cool to see my name in the *Guinness Book of World Records*, a book I read regularly as a kid? Absolutely. But my main reason for breaking the record was to open doors to share my faith and motivate people not to give up no matter what challenges they face. And that has happened. I've been in schools, churches, sports awards banquets, safety seminars, graduation ceremonies, and businesses across the country and around the world demonstrating my golf swing and sharing my story. I've seen people encouraged, motivated, and inspired. More importantly, I've seen countless people confess faith in Jesus.

So, no, my name never got into that book. But the purpose was never to make my name known. It was to introduce more people to Him.

[If you are interested in booking me for an event of any kind, you can do so by visiting my website, **www.jeffbardel.com**, or by emailing me at **booking@jeffbardel.com**.]

CHAPTER 18

My Challenge for You

Writing this book has been a long process. A very long process. The first time I started it, I had a catastrophic hard drive failure. I lost the first three chapters that had taken me months to write. I not only lost everything I'd written, I lost my entire laptop. It ended up in the trash. After getting a new laptop, I started working on it again. Thankfully I'd sent the first chapter to a few friends to get their honest opinions, and one still had it buried in his inbox. After making some tweaks to that chapter, I started again, this time from chapter two.

About a year or so later and five chapters into the book, I hopped on my laptop to bang out a few more pages. I opened up the folder to retrieve the book and the folder was empty. *Nothing to worry about,* I thought. *I'm sure it's here somewhere.*

I asked my wife if she moved it to a different folder. She hadn't. I searched my Recent Documents folder and there were a few listed, but my book wasn't one of them. Weird. I typed in the name of my document into the search bar and hit search. Nothing was found. Now I was starting to get a little stressed.

A call to a buddy who works in the IT field calmed my fears when he told me he'd take a look. "Nobody deleted the document, so it has to be there," I kept telling myself. "It didn't just disappear."

I dropped my laptop off at my friend's house and waited for the good news. He searched, poked, prodded, kicked, stomped, threw, elbowed, kneed, kneaded, baptized, exercised, and exorcised my computer to no avail. It was gone...again. That hurt. Yes, I was only five chapters in, but there were days I'd start from the first page and reread what I'd written, make some tweaks, do complete rewrites, delete sections, and add new content. Yes, I was only five chapters in, but I'd written those five chapters at least five times. Years of work was gone. I had to take a break and regroup.

I'm not sure how long my hiatus lasted, but it wasn't short. I was mad. I probably had a pity party or two. On occasion, I'd open my laptop and search for the document again, but it was gone. I'd close the laptop and walk away.

Was I even supposed to write the book? I wondered. *Is it worth all of this?*

HECK YES IT IS! I finally concluded. I'd faced and overcome a lot bigger obstacles in life than losing my book twice.

Lost my arm. Overcame it!

Battled depression. Overcame it!

Contemplated suicide. Overcame it!

"Golf is a hard enough game with two arms. I can't even imagine trying to play with one. Maybe you should stop trying now before it gets too frustrating." Overcame it!

#TEACHABLEMOMENT
How Big is Your 'Want To?'

I wish I had a dollar for every time someone saw me hit a golf ball with one arm and said, "That is really impressive. I could never do that." And while I appreciate the compliment, I always answer, "If you wanted it bad enough you could!"

For the most part, they are right. They could never hit a golf ball like I do with one arm, but it's not because I'm that good with one. It's because they have two. They could try to learn to hit a ball like I do, but when things got tough, they could always swing with two. If I was going to be able to play golf, I had to learn to play with one arm. I had no other option. Too often, a second, easier option can rob us of what we really want. We have to ask ourselves if we are willing to go through the painful process to get what we really want or are we just going to settle for something less. And by painful, I don't necessarily mean physical pain. It could be the pain of going the extra mile when doing "just enough" would suffice. It could be the pain of continuing to seek knowledge about a subject on your own time instead of vegging out in front of the tv for the night. It really depends on the size of your 'want to.'

When I first became interested in golf, my 'want to' was big enough that I learned to play. My 'want to' was also big enough to continue to improve. My 'want to' is big enough now that I still continue to improve. I will stop improving the day I reach the limit of my 'want to.' Because as long as I want to get better, I will continue to put in the practice, I will continue to seek advice, and I will continue striving to improve.

Throughout my life, I have progressed in every area of my life as much as my 'want to.' At my jobs. With my friendships. In my marriage. As a father. As a preacher. As a motivational and safety speaker. In my personal growth. In my relationship with God. Once I reach the end of my 'want to' in a certain area, I will, at best, plateau, if not regress toward that subject.

A goal of mine for the longest time was to run a marathon. I've always enjoyed running, so I wanted to take it to the limit of running 26.2 miles. So I started working toward it, researching how to train, running regularly, but taking rest days to allow my body to recover. Things were going well and my stamina was improving, but I started experiencing pain in my left knee. I tried to run through it for a few days, but it kept getting worse. Taking the advice of some other runners, I took some time off to recover. A week later when I ran, I felt great. But in two weeks, the knee pain was back.

I was told it could be my running shoes that was causing the issue. So I went to one of those fancy stores where they videotape you running on a treadmill and then give you options on which shoe is best for you. I ended up with a pair of gray and purple Mizuno Wave Rider 12s. I loved running in them. They were so light it felt like I was running in socks. I was thankful that I could pound the pavement in a shoe that could help alleviate my knee pain. But in two weeks, the pain was back yet again. Eventually, I ended up in a knee brace and had regular cortisone shots to relieve the pain and inflammation. Years later, I went under the knife because the pain became unbearable. Dealing with all of this, I reached the end of my 'want to' to run a marathon. And, to this day, I have progressed no further toward running a marathon. In fact, I've regressed, because my stamina has decreased dramatically since then. (I'm not saying my 'want to' in this area won't come back, but it's currently not there.)

So I'll ask you, how big is your 'want to' in various areas of your life? Are you happy with where you are on your job or do you want to get promoted? If you want a promotion, what are you doing to get it? Are you just hoping someone notices you or are you doing something to stand apart from the rest? Are you working hard or just working hard enough? At two of my last jobs, I started each of them as a part-time employee. The job market was tough so I was willing to work anywhere they would hire me. On one job, I was given favorable shifts within no time because of my work ethic. My boss put his arm around me one day and said, "Have I told you how glad I am that I hired you?" On my other job, I received three promotions in a two-year time span. I went from part-time to a full-time employee with a salary and benefits because I separated myself from my coworkers by working hard and going the extra mile.

Are you happy with your marriage or do you want to have a better one? Even if you have a good marriage, do you want a great one? If so, what steps are you taking to make that happen? I regularly ask my wife how I'm doing as a husband

> and what areas I can improve. I have to set my feelings aside because my marriage is way more important than potentially getting my feelings hurt or getting defensive. (I also ask my girls how I'm doing as a dad and how I can improve. It's better to ask than to just assume you're doing well.)
>
> Are you content in your relationship with God or do you want to know Him more? One guarantee I can 100 percent tell you is you have as close of a relationship with God as you want. Period. End of story. You determine how much time you read the Bible. You determine how much time you pray. You determine how often you worship. Out of the few examples I've listed in this teachable moment, this is the one you have the most control over. On your job, you can go above and beyond all of your coworkers and still get overlooked for a promotion. In your marriage, you can do everything in your power to be the best spouse you can possibly be, but it doesn't guarantee your spouse will reciprocate. But if you want a deeper and closer relationship with God, you will absolutely get it. Jeremiah 29:3 (NLT) says, "If you look for me wholeheartedly, you will find me," and 1 Chronicles 28:9 (NLT) says, "If you seek him, you will find him." There are no "probablys" or "maybes" in either of those verses. If you legitimately want to know God more, seek Him and you will absolutely find Him.
>
> So, again, I'll ask you, how big is your 'want to' in different aspects of your life? If you want more, do something to make it happen!

Lost my book twice? Overcame it, obviously, as you are holding a copy in your hand right now.

But as I look back, I'm not convinced that losing my book twice wasn't an absolute blessing. Yes, it was *extremely* frustrating to put in all of that work and then have it disappear twice, but something happened recently that I think is the perfect way to end this book. If I never lost what I'd already written, the book would have gone to print before this experience I'm about to tell you.

As I've mentioned once or twice in this book, aside from being a preacher and motivational speaker, I also conduct safety seminars. My goal is in the telling of my story it will help others work more safely and avoid a horrible work injury like I experienced. Over the years, I have had the opportunity to conduct two safety seminars at the factory where I lost my arm. The last one I did, something happened that I will remember for the rest of my life.

It was going to be a long two days. Because of the number of employees and the three shifts they worked at the glass making facility, I would be doing *a lot* of seminars. I would do two the first night, and six on day two. On my two-hour drive to the plant, I prayed a prayer that was rather unusual. It kind of came to me out of nowhere.

"Lord, I know these are safety seminars, so I'm not allowed to talk about You, but I'm asking for an opportunity to lead someone to Jesus. In Jesus name. Amen."

That was it. That was the extent of my prayer. Many times people think prayer has to be this long, drawn out thing where you beg and plead for something to happen. I'm not saying all of my prayers are this short, but this time I knew I asked God for something that He wanted just as bad as I did, and it was in line with His Word.

The first day actually started at 11:15 p.m. when I spoke to half of the third-shift crew. After my 45-minute presentation and a 15-minute break to allow the employees to get back to their work stations to relieve their coworkers, the other half of third shift came to the conference room for my last session of day one, starting at 12:15 a.m. I was in my car an hour later making the 15-minute drive to my parent's house, the same house they lived in the day I lost my arm, where I would crash for the night before an early alarm would wake me and send me back to the factory that morning.

Day two was rather uneventful until my fifth session. In each seminar, I walked the employees through every step of my accident and followed with some training, precautions, and steps that could produce a safer work environment. As I was retelling the story in my penultimate session, I reached the part where I was standing in front of the office window after I'd run bleeding from my accident site. I said, "There were some guys in the office and one came out and tackled me to the ground."

As soon as I said that, a big, meaty hand on the back row shot up. I hadn't asked a question, so I had no idea why this guy was raising his hand. He had my attention though, so I paused and looked at him.

A gravelly voice boomed, "That was me!"

I stood there shocked. I was looking at one of the guys who played a role in saving my life. I'd always wondered who ran out of the office to help me that day, but I'd never thought to ask. In my mind I made a mental note: *I want to talk to that guy when this session is over.* I thanked him for what he did that day and continued my presentation, but I was excited to talk to him and see what he remembered about that day 24 years prior.

When the session ended, a group of people approached me and thanked me for what I'd shared. A few shared their condolences because it was the first time they'd seen me since my dad had passed away. But then the strangest thing happened. The room emptied except for me and one other person.

That was unusual because out of the seven seminars I'd conducted to that point, people milled around in the conference room after every single session for at least 10 minutes. But within two or three minutes, everyone had left the room except for me and the guy who'd raised his hand.

He approached me and I shook his hand. He introduced himself as Joe Dew, the same man I introduced to you back in chapter three. He said everybody called him Mountain Dew. I asked if he liked the drink a lot or if it was because he was a rather large man, standing at six feet tall but weighing in around 260. He told me it wasn't anything creative like that, but simply a play on his last name.

After sharing a few pleasantries, I asked him what he remembered about that day, a lot of which I shared with you back in chapter three. One statement he made echoed on the inside of me for some reason. He said, "I remember being covered in your blood."

I was surprised how much my accident still seemed to affect him. I took the opportunity to apologize for putting him through that. In fact, everyone I've talked to in the writing of this book who I worked with the day of my accident, I apologized for putting them through that trauma. Many of them, including myself, spent numerous months (or longer) in counseling. I never knew my accident had lasting effects on them.

Joe asked if I had time for him to share a story with me.

"You helped save my life," I said. "I've got all the time in the world."

The story he shared with me had my jaw on the floor. Almost 10 months to the day after my accident, Joe experienced a hellish accident that still makes me cringe, even after everything I've been through.

They were rebuilding one of the furnaces in the hot end. A furnace is basically a steel frame lined on the inside with refractory brick because of its ability to withstand extremely high temperatures. Rebuilding a furnace requires removing all of the old brick and replacing it with new ones. After putting the new bricks in place, it takes three weeks to heat the furnace back up to it's full 2850 degrees because as the bricks heat up they expand, so bolts holding the steel frame together have to be loosened to allow for the expansion of the bricks.

The temperature on the furnace was up to 1600 degrees and the bolts needed to be loosened again. When Joe stepped out onto the boards above the furnace to loosen the bolts, he didn't know one of the supporting boards had been moved. He felt the board crack and knew something was wrong.

"The board collapsed and I fell into the furnace," Joe told me. "The fire back-draft shot up through the hole I just fell through."

He described the feeling of being in the furnace as sheer torture. He gripped his stomach with both hands and felt his skin and flesh melting off of his body. In a panic, he started pounding the walls of glowing red bricks surrounding him, desperately fighting to get out and save his life. But each time he pounded the wall, more of his flesh stuck to his brick cell.

He estimated with the furnace completely empty, it was about eight feet deep, so climbing out wasn't an option, especially when everything he touched melted his skin. He saw the hand of a coworker shoot through the hole he'd fallen through. Joe grabbed his coworker's arm and felt hope for a split second as he was lifted from the ground, but he was quickly dropped. His coworker's shoulder dislocated trying to lift Joe's from his fiery enclosure because he estimated his weight to be closer to 320 pounds at the time.

"When he dropped me, my heart sank and I thought to myself, *This is it*," Joe recalled, thinking his life was over.

He doesn't know how long he was inside the furnace, but it felt like forever. A few seconds later, another hand appeared through the hole in the board above his head. Joe's hand swallowed the wrist protruding toward him. The man's hand gripped Joe's wrist, and the next thing Joe remembers was flying back through the hole and landing with a thud on the concrete, his shirt and pants still engulfed in flames. The man who freed Joe from his torturous cage was barely half his size, weighing around 170 pounds.

Over the next six months, Joe had three skin graft surgeries to replace all of the skin from his left breast to his left knee and had 159 large staples in his stomach area alone. Within eight months, he was back at work.

It's rare for me to hear of an injury as tragic as mine, so I was mesmerized by every word out of Joe's mouth. He kept harping on the guy who freed him from the furnace, saying he had to look like a cartoon character the way he was snatched off the ground and thrown through the air by someone half his size.

He said, "I've never felt power like that in a human being. That wasn't him. That was the hand of God that rescued me."

The next thing he said really caught my attention.

"I don't know why God let me live that day."

As those words came out of his mouth, I knew the prayer I prayed on my drive to the safety seminar was about to be answered—"Lord, I know these are safety seminars, so I'm not allowed to talk about You, but I'm asking for an opportunity to lead someone to Jesus. In Jesus name. Amen."

I responded to Joe by saying, "I do."

He said, "You do?"

I told him, "I definitely do." I followed by telling him a lot of the content you've read in this book, how when I had my accident I knew *about* God, but didn't know Him through His Son, Jesus. I told him how a stranger invited me to church and I gave my life to Jesus. I then asked him if it was okay for me to ask him a personal question. He nodded in the affirmative.

"Joe, if anything were to happen to me today, I know I would go to Heaven to spend eternity with Jesus. Can you say the same thing?"

He bowed his head and shook it slowly from side to side. I heard a soft, "No." He added that he never felt comfortable in church because he didn't own a suit.

I said, "We can take care of that right now. Jesus died on the cross for you to save you from your sins. All you have to do is admit you're a sinner, believe that Jesus rose from the dead, and you will be saved. I can pray with you right now. Would you want to do that?"

He lifted his head and tears were running down his cheeks. "I'd like that."

So, standing in the back of the empty conference room, my new friend, Joe Dew, prayed to ask Jesus to be his personal Lord and Savior for the first time in his life at the age of 65. His name was added to the Lamb's Book of Life.

Twenty four years earlier in the same factory, Joe was covered in my blood. That day, he was covered by the blood of Jesus!

He played a key role in saving my life 24 years before, and that day, God allowed me to play a role in saving his life for eternity!

My friend, if you've ever accepted Jesus as your Lord and Savior, you have the absolute best news the world will ever hear. And you know what? *The world needs to hear it!* And you don't have to be a preacher to do so.

I planned on writing out a long teaching about why you should share your faith with others (maybe that will be my next book), but I'm going to simplify it. Jesus told you to in all four gospels (Matt. 28:19, Mark 16:15, Luke 24:46–47, and John 20:19–21), so do it! Easy enough?

I know it can bring fear or cause you to be nervous, but we need to understand that our fear and nervousness in sharing our faith isn't nearly as important as someone's eternity! I'm going to say that again for the people in the back. *Our fear and nervousness in sharing our faith isn't nearly as important as someone's eternity!*

I challenge you to pray for opportunities to share Jesus with other people. I promise you God will answer your prayer because He loves each and every person on the face of this earth more than you or I ever will.

Much like Joe Dew's coworker reached in and snatched him out of that fiery furnace, you can reach into somebody's life and snatch them out of the pit of Hell and introduce them to a better life with Jesus!

In the past, I've prayed for God to send Christians across the paths of my friends and family members to lead them to Jesus. Those prayers were often answered. But did you ever think that maybe, just maybe, *you* are the answer to someone's prayer to lead their friend or family member to Jesus?

If you want to support the ministry as we
travel leading people to Jesus,
you can do so by visiting
www.jeffbardel.com/support
to set up a recurring gift or to give
a one-time donation.

All donations are tax-deductible.